TRACER!

TRACER!
THE SEARCH FOR MISSING PERSONS
ED GOLDFADER

NASH PUBLISHING
LOS ANGELES

Copyright © 1970 by Nash Publishing
All rights reserved. No part of this book
may be reproduced in any form or by any means
without permission in writing from the publisher.
Library of Congress Catalog Number: 72-107861
Standard Book Number: 8402-1134-1
Published simultaneously in the United States and
Canada by NASH PUBLISHING, 9255 Sunset Boulevard,
Los Angeles, California 90069
Printed in the United States of America

Current printing (last digit):
10 9 8 7 6 5 4 3 2 1

FOR PAULA, LAURA,
DAVID AND ELLEN

CONTENTS

1
HOW DO YOU KNOW?
PAGE 1

2
HOW'D YOU GET INTO THIS BUSINESS, ANYWAY?
PAGE 17

3
A CASE OF IDENTITY
PAGE 29

4
AS SANE AS I AM
PAGE 41

INTERLUDE I
PAGE 53

5
THE FINISH LINE
PAGE 57

6
THE ENTIRELY MISSING PERSON
PAGE 67

7
NO PATTERN
PAGE 77

8
DON'T TAKE ANY WOODEN INDIANS
PAGE 85

INTERLUDE II
PAGE 93

9
HOW COULD SHE DO THIS TO US?
PAGE 97

10
AS SIMPLE AS THAT
PAGE 107

11
HAPPY ANNIVERSARY
PAGE 115

12
A NICE DULL JOB
PAGE 123

INTERLUDE III
PAGE 135

13
MONEY, MONEY, WHO WANTS MONEY?
PAGE 139

14
THE REALLY EVIL PEOPLE
PAGE 151

15
ONE IN A MILLION
PAGE 163

INTERLUDE IV
PAGE 175

16
I'LL COME BACK FOR YOU
PAGE 179

17
THE IMPOSSIBLE SITUATION
PAGE 193

EPILOGUE

TRACER!

1
HOW DO YOU KNOW?

Mrs. Halliday called to tell me that her husband had left the very small town from which he'd sent her the postcard. She'd had the postcard, as I knew, the day before. I thought about that for a second or so, and told her Mr. Halliday would be in touch with her within forty-eight hours. I said he was on his way back to her, twenty-seven days after having "deserted" her. Naturally, she asked me one question:

"How do you know?"

Equally naturally, I couldn't tell her.

I meet a lot of people, one way and another, and, whenever anyone finds out what I do for a living, the same question—or a very slight variation of it—pops up, as if all those people were so many automatic toasters.

The trouble—part of the trouble, anyway—is that the answer takes a lot of time. Maybe in this book I can resolve it at last.

You see, Mrs. Halliday had placed the search for her husband with me six days before that telephone call. And, of course, she thought I'd been working to find her husband for six days.

She was wrong. I'd been working on it for nearly twenty years.

And . . . twenty years can take a bit of time to talk about.

So, now, with a bundle of pages to fill, perhaps I'll finally find the time. I hope that at least some of the people who've asked me that question will take some time of their own to read this; because if the answer isn't here, I probably can't provide it at all.

To start with, though, let's get back to the Hallidays. . . .

Peter Halliday (according to the story Mrs. Halliday told when she paid her first visit to Tracers Company) had been growing more and more restless over the previous few months. The Hallidays had been married fourteen years, and "Peter always did have these spells of restlessness, you know, so I didn't really think too much of it this time," Mrs. Halliday told me. But this time was, she went on, different: this time, Peter had found something to keep the spark of restlessness burning.

He'd dropped in at a bar with which he'd grown more and more familiar as his restlessness grew. The bar was in the town where Peter lived—a town called Suburbia (not its right name of course, but then Peter Halliday isn't *his* right name either). He'd run into an acquaintance he hadn't seen in years, a man named Walter Knapp.

Walter was a new arrival in Suburbia, and he had a vague notion of getting some sort of job as a systems analyst with a nearby electronics company. The notion wasn't any better than vague: Walter was distinctly the footloose type, having held quite a long list of jobs since Peter Halliday had last seen him.

They'd been shipmates on a destroyer during World War II, and (as they both remembered it, through the double haze of twenty-five years and the bottoms of a growing number of empty glasses) they'd had a wonderful time. Best part of their lives, they assured each other solemnly; even the Murmansk run had been adventurous, and there were other ports—ports stocked with gaudy memories. Best time of his life, Peter decided, and Walter agreed with him as if the fact were so natural it needed no argument at all.

What was more, Walter had gone right on in much the same way, with much the same life-style. He was, by his own somewhat colorful description, a wanderer, responsible to nobody but himself, footloose and fancy-free. Why, he'd been—just about everywhere, he went on (as his old buddy's enthusiasm and the steady flow of drinks colored and enlarged the more pleasant events in his memory). Been everywhere, seen everything . . . a great life, Pete. Nothing like it, believe me.

And so the hours, on that last night, went by.

Peter, through the foggy, subdued excitement that grew up as he relived that colorful past and Walter's equally colorful present, toyed with the thought of inviting Walter home. But he knew he didn't really want to do that. The combination of *Walter* and *home* just did not go together. Not in the least.

On the other hand. . .

Walter was revolving a glass between his hands. "What've you been doing lately?" he asked.

"Who, me?" Peter blinked, bringing his mind slowly back to a focus on the dull everyday world. What did he have to offer, after all, that matched Walter's colorful tales? "Oh . . . nothing much. Nothing much. Working." He took a swallow of his own drink. "In the city, you know? Living out here, working in the city. Nothing much."

Walter nodded wisely, as if he understood every detail of the Halliday life. "Married?" he asked, and went on to answer his own question: "Sure—you must be, by now. Almost everybody is."

Almost everybody . . . sure, Peter thought, all the dull people, living their dull lives. Not the footloose, fancy-free. . . . "Hell, no," he said, and, hearing himself say that much, began to get a series of absolutely new and shiny and wonderful ideas. "I'm as single as you are. Singler. At least." Another drink. "Me, married? That's a laugh. Single: that's me, Walt. A great life, single."

The whole idea was balanced in his mind, shimmering there like a mirage. But it was no mirage, Peter assured himself; it was real. It was his future—new, and shiny, and just about perfect. Vaguely, he realized that Walter was talking. "Well, I thought only married guys lived out here," he was saying. "Single guys in the city. I mean, out here there's all those married types, you know what I mean: their wives and kids, and the lawns to take care of, crabgrass and all like that, and these wives and kids. . . ." He made a sketchy gesture with the hand holding his current drink, and miraculously didn't spill any of it.

Wives and kids. . . . Peter thought of his ten-year-old daughter. She'd had a birthday party the other day. Pretty good party, too. Ronnie . . . well, he'd match Ronnie up with any ten-year-old in Suburbia. Or anywhere. Sure he would.

But that was his *old* life. It was gone now. The new life, the free life, was about to begin.

"Well, I'm not here for long," he said, as casually as he could. "Just for a little while, I mean. Not long at all. In fact . . . in fact. . . ." He looked around him. Nobody but Walter was listening. That was right; that was the smart way to play it. "I've been thinking, Walt. Should be about time to move on, you know? Tired of this place. Might be time to move on." He pondered that for a minute or two. "Out West, maybe. Go West, young man—might be time, Walt. Been thinking about it." He tried to look like a man who'd been thinking about it.

Walter certainly seemed interested.(A lot of the interest might have been just because Peter Halliday was buying the drinks, but Peter was beyond even considering anything like that.) "Yeah?" Walter said.

"What's going on out West that's so great?"

It was not an easy question. "Well," Peter said very slowly indeed, "it's—well, it's different, Walt. You know. *Different.*"

Walter apparently thought that over and found an idea or two in it. "Change of luck," he sort of mumbled to himself. Why, in the East they were slave drivers, that's all, just slave drivers. But out West . . . out West, now, I hear the government-contract boys out there are just plain hungry for good men. "Don't have to work yourself half to death out there," he said. "And lots of good openings . . . lot's of 'em. All over."

"Right," Peter chimed in. "Couldn't be righter"—just as if he knew something about the comparative demands for systems analysts all over the country. He nodded once or twice, feeling scared, expectant and solemn all at once. "Listen, Walt—"

"What?"

"Well. . . ." There was quite a long pause. Peter had to nerve himself up to get the words out, though they were the right words, he told himself. The *right* words. "Well, listen, Walt: why don't we go?"

But Walter hadn't, perhaps, been following the conversation with any great clarity. Perhaps he was thinking about the appointment for a job interview he had scheduled for the morning. Perhaps he just thought that his old pal was simply building a nice, colorful fantasy it might be time to drop out of. And perhaps he had enough liquor in him by then so that the moment of time he happened to be in was the only important moment there could ever be. "Go?" he asked. "Where—

out West?"

Peter, having heard himself say the words, went with them in a wild determined decision. Call it momentum. "Sure," he said. "Why not?"

For a brief couple of seconds, Walter Knapp seemed to sober up. "You mean," he said, very slowly, "right now... just pack up and leave? Just like that?"

It occurs to me that there must be hundreds, even thousands, of such conversations in bars across the country, every year. No doubt very few of them go any farther than simple talk, and a fair percentage are forgotten entirely when the next morning, complete with throbbing head, rolls round. But Peter Halliday's talk with Walter Knapp was one of the few that had immediate consequences, for reasons I'm not entirely sure I can figure out—and for reasons any psychoanalyst would be happy to charge a Peter Halliday two or three thousand dollars to invent.

By the time one more drink had been poured over the decision, it seemed not only sensible but inevitable. And Knapp's car was conveniently right outside.

Peter had left his home, choosing to walk the less-than-half-a-mile to the bar. So the two men rode back to Peter's house within a very few minutes. Peter went in, moving quietly. He threw some things into a single suitcase, hunted up all the loose cash he could find (a total amounting to a good deal more than the fifty dollars those people in the ads always used to advise you not to carry more than), and, as softly as possible, closed the door behind him. He climbed into his own car, complete with suitcase and money; he backed it out of the driveway; and he followed Walter's car down the street—and right on out of Suburbia, heading West.

Mrs. Halliday, as it happened, had been no more than lightly asleep when the two old shipmates made temporary port in front of the house. She'd heard her husband come in, and she'd heard him leave again. She'd heard the car being started, heard it backing out of the driveway. But none of that sounded really unusual. She imagined he'd decided to go for a drive—something he often did when in a restless mood—and something no amount of argument about the dangers of drinking-plus-driving had ever stopped him from doing.

She went to the window, just in time to see Peter's car pulling away, right behind another car. Patiently, dozing on and off through the night, she waited for his return.

She called the local hospitals, and then the police, at noon the next day.

And, a little more than two weeks later, she came to Tracers Company.

At the time Mrs. Halliday finished telling me her story, I knew almost nothing of what you've just read. I knew about Walter Knapp. I knew Peter had met him in a bar, and for all the good it did me, I knew which bar. I also knew they'd driven off one behind the other. Between Mrs. Halliday's having noticed the two cars and a police check, I had that much.

I knew, too, that Peter had two credit cards in his wallet, and I knew the license number of his car. As for Walter Knapp's car—well, it was just one of those things. It seems nobody, not even Mrs. Halliday, had happened to notice so much as which state it was registered in. It was a car, and that was about all I had on that front.

I knew about Peter's restlessness; and I knew one more important fact. He'd managed to stay lost, despite earnest searching, for over two weeks. And that, in this country and in these times, is by no means as easy as you might think.

Of course, the obvious loopholes could be plugged. Peter might use his credit cards. He might, somewhere along the way, abandon his car. (The car, if found, would at least have given us a fair notion of the direction he was heading in. As things turned out, by the way, it had been abandoned, and was found—but not until the day before Peter arrived home. By then, of course, anything we might have gotten from it simply wasn't needed.)

Going one step further: if Peter Halliday wanted to get very, very fancy about his disappearance, he might have decided to grow a moustache, buy a pair of plainglass spectacles, adopt a new haircomb or disguise himself in any number of ways. You can probably invent six or seven more for yourself.

None of that would have done him much good. It is, simply, not very easy to disappear.

For one thing, sooner or later you are going to need money. Sell your car—and the papers evidencing the sale will remain and provide a trace. Get a job—and you're going to have to get a false Social Security number. (And that, believe me, creates a good many more problems than it solves.)

But, most importantly, there's this: you are going to remain *you*.

A man whose long-time hobby is skiing, for instance, will probably not be found hiding out in the middle of Kansas. A man who collected stamps before he vanished will probably show up, sooner or later, at a stamp auction—or will write for a rare stamp advertised in a magazine devoted to such matters. It is a lot easier to change jobs than it is to change the life-long accumulation of habits, hobbies and interests we all carry around with us. You're not likely to find a bookworm trying to climb Mount Everest.

The considerations just noted suggest, of course, a great many lines of inquiry. Most of them, however, take much longer than six days to run through. And my job isn't simply to find people.

My job is to find people as quickly as possible.

So, though we started some normal procedures, I was depending on something else. We got to work checking automobile sales within a reasonable radius of Suburbia. We instituted a watch on Peter Halliday's credit cards. We started running three or four other simple investigative lines.

And we waited.

Because, from what Mrs. Halliday had told me, I knew one thing. I was depending on Peter Halliday to help us find him—and I was more than reasonably sure that he was going to do us the favor.

11 How Do You Know?

The fact is that quite a lot of people really do want to disappear. Some of them even manage to do just that. But very, very few of them want to disappear for good—or even for very long. Peter, clearly, was not one of those few.

After a pull-out as rapid and as careless as his had been (well, his wife, after all, *had* been awakened; he hadn't even bothered to check that; he hadn't waited one extra day, not even to get more cash together; he was, at least to begin with, using his own car; he took only one suitcase and whatever clothes he happened to grab in the dark house)—after that, there's a short first period of elation, when everything seems just great. You've made it after all! You're free! You can start life all over again, with no responsibilities!

Then reality starts creeping in.

The footloose life, as described by Walter Knapp in a hazy barroom conversation, is not quite as great when you're actually out there living it. There are advantages to a home and family when the alternative is a rented room, a lumpy mattress, and four very close dull walls. There are advantages to friends and neighbors when everyone around you is a stranger.

And, most important of all: the life you left *is,* and usually remains, the life you really want to live. You chose it—and probably not all at once over a flock of drinks at the local bar.

You go right on being you. And. . . .

Well, let's say your wife's small talk bothers you. If so, the small talk of every waitress, saleswoman, stewardess and cashier will bother you just as much, and probably a good deal more—you haven't had the time to immunize yourself to it.

Sooner or later, then, Peter Halliday was going to make the move that couldn't be missed. The easy way to find Peter Halliday—and the fast way—was to let Peter Halliday to the job—and then follow up, if necessary.

Sooner or later. . . . In the Halliday case, it was a postcard, addressed to his wife. It said: "Don't worry—I'm doing fine! Pete." No return address, but a postmark pinning it down to a small town in Colorado. (And when I say small I mean small: it doesn't even show up in the average atlas.)

I told Mrs. Halliday that I was sending our nearest man to the town; she insisted that she wanted to go along too.

And I couldn't really talk her out of it. It was possible that Peter had remained in the town. It wasn't probable (they don't usually make it *that* simple) but I couldn't give her a flat negative on it.

In any case, if he'd left, there were only a few simple questions to ask. I arranged for Mrs. Halliday to rendezvous with our man.

Next day, they called me.

Peter wasn't there any longer—as figured. But he hadn't gone unnoticed, not in a town that size. He'd gone into the local store-*cum*-post-office, bought his postcard and borrowed the postmaster's fountain pen (explaining that "these new-fangled ballpoints don't work as good").

After writing the card, he'd absentmindedly

pocketed the pen and walked out. Just as the postmaster reached the front door, the car took off. It was heading East—in a general sort of way, back toward Suburbia.

The postmaster gave our man and Mrs. Halliday a good description of the car, including license-plate number and state of issue. That gave us a line on Walter Knapp's car, but, as I explained to Mrs. Halliday, we didn't need it.

In fact, Mrs. Halliday (who had bad air connections back: she couldn't get a flight until late the following day) barely arrived home within my forty-eight-hour time limit.

She beat Peter back to Suburbia by a bit more than four hours.

A superman, I am not. I'm not always right to the hour, or even to the day. But it's perfectly possible for me to boast that I know more about Peter Halliday—whom I have not met to this day—than Peter Halliday may know about himself. It works like this:

On the basis of no more than the speed and carelessness of his departure, I could begin with the assumption that he was following a pattern I've grown very familiar with. On the (further) basis of the postcard—which bore no obvious message of great importance for the recipient (except that it showed Mrs. Halliday her husband was still alive)—I could see that the assumption was still holding, and I could really start to depend on it.

No, it didn't have to be forty-eight hours, on the nose. But if it had been more than twice that, I'd have begun to worry. I'd have begun to wonder . . . and not only about Peter Halliday, and the possibility that he'd smacked the car into the side of a mountain, or the like.

I'd have begun to wonder, too, about Walter Knapp.

The pattern—the simple runaway pattern Peter undoubtedly thought was all his own invention—is so standard that I could rest on the assurance that Peter was not going to disappear for good. Not on his own. So, if he did, the logical place to start would have been with the only other person in the original picture: Walter.

Suppose, for instance, that the two men had gone on drinking and, sooner or later, had found themselves in a fight. And suppose that, when the fight was finally over, Walter didn't have much choice: he *had* to make Peter, or what was left of Peter, disappear.

It didn't happen, not in the Halliday case. Nor did it worry me very much; that, too, as the pattern told me, was reasonably unlikely.

The pattern, you see, was holding all the way into Colorado. If there was to have been a fight, the odds were that it would have happened long, long before the postcard had ever been sent. And if Peter had been "disappeared," so to speak, he certainly hadn't sent the postcard. . . .

Besides all which, there was so sign of Walter Knapp in that Colorado town.

No; there was no need to worry over Walter Knapp. Remember that, by the time he got to Colorado, Peter was on his way *back*.

(Incidentally, the loose end did tie itself up, in case you're wondering. Walter Knapp called the Halliday home—from California—a week after Peter's return. He wanted to know whether his old pal had made it back O.K., and whether he had sold the car yet, and, if so, where was the money. That is all I ever knew about the call, or about subsequent relationships between Walter and the Hallidays; your guess is as good as mine, from there on in.)

Peter Halliday, as I've explained, striking out in quest of a taste of freedom and individuality, was following a simple and very familiar route. I've been getting to know that route for some twenty years, while Peter had very little time either to get accustomed to it, or to improvise on it.

As simple, in other words, as that.

There are, of course, the times you have to guard against: the times the pattern breaks, the times a new twist (or, anyhow, a twist new to me) shows up.

And I'm always learning new things about people, and the ways they act, and the various ways there are to find them when necessary. So maybe, after all, that original question—this title's chapter, and the question I get about as often as a writer gets: "Where do you get those ideas?" or a resident of Hollywood gets: "Is it really true that . . .?" —never can, finally, once and for all, find itself an answer.

All I can do—and what, among other things, the rest of this book is going to try to do—is to attempt to give a description of the learning process.

The oddities . . . the novelties . . . the things you learn, and the things you tell yourself you always ought to have known. . .

Call it (if you absolutely have to call it something) *the answer, so far.*

But I'm at least as conscious as you are of the fact that there's likely to be a somewhat different answer next year, when I learn some more, when some more odd things have happened.

Next year . . . or next week. . .

Or tomorrow.

2
HOW'D YOU GET INTO THIS BUSINESS, ANYWAY?

Now there, believe me, is another familiar question. Nobody seems to ask an accountant how he got to be an accountant . . . but a private investigator? That's different. It seems to be an odd occupation, as far as a lot of people are concerned. How did I get into it, anyway? Where (in other words) did all the answers start?

And when did I begin to learn the difference between the way the private eye operates in the movies, on TV, in the thousands and thousands of detective novels and mystery magazines . . . and the way things really are?

When I get right down to it, I think that's a question the fiction writers don't seem to get around to much: how does their private eye get to be a private eye? I suppose there may be an exception floating around somewhere; but, offhand, I'd be willing to make a bet that none of the exceptions, even, started out in a dentist's waiting-room—using, for a main prop, an out-of-date magazine.

It just isn't very dramatic that way, I suppose; it's hardly the sort of thing that would occur to an imaginative writer, and, if it did, it's hardly the sort of thing he'd get all eager to follow through on.

But the real world is under absolutely no obligation to be as dramatic as the movies, or TV . . . and, if I'm going to go back to the beginning, I'm afraid we're going to have to start with that waiting-room—and, to be entirely exact, with a college football game I'd played in, the Saturday before.

Away back in prehistoric days . . . 1950, to be exact. . . .

Back then, football helmets were minus the faceguard contraption you see on them today. (The equipment manager did get orders to put one on your helmet—if you managed somehow, to break your nose; but he also had orders to remove it in two weeks, which was, it was assumed, time enough for the break to have healed.) On an otherwise beautiful New England autumn Saturday afternoon that season, I very cleverly managed to trap the elbow of the fast-moving and efficient middle guard playing opposite me by catching it

19 How'd You Get Into This Business, Anyway?

square in my mouth. By Monday morning, some of the aching had gone, but my smile looked both uncertain and decidedly gray. The team doctor took one look and made an appointment for me to see an oral surgeon in Boston. I think I heard him say something about—now, what was that?—"root-canal work."

I look back with great admiration on my own unbelievable bravery: I kept the appointment.

So there I was, sitting in the waiting-room, looking around for something to keep my mind off words like "root-canal work." And of course there are always piles of magazines in dentists' offices, magazines going right on back to the date the dentist began his practice. In fact, I've sometimes had the suspicion that they inherit older magazines from even older dentists who are about to retire.

Anyhow . . . I began riffling through the pages of one of those magazines, and an article caught my attention. It was about an organization called Skip Tracers Company.

Skip Tracers Company was in the business of tracking down missing people, the article said, and it went on to give all sorts of interesting details about how they worked for corporations who were interested in locating stockholders who apparently didn't know that the stock they held had any value. Interesting to me, anyhow. . . .

Not that the article stopped there; by no means. It went on to talk about other people Skip Tracers Company found: debtors being tracked down by creditors; witnesses to wills, witnesses to accidents; runaways of all sorts, ranging from the husband or wife who decided that his or her talents would be more appreciated elsewhere (people like Peter Halliday, for instance) to teenagers who just weren't up to facing the folks when the bad report card came through—and just about everything in between.

Skip Tracers Company, at that time, had been in business for over twenty years. Its headquarters were in New York.

And...

The receptionist tapped me on the shoulder, is what happened then. I put the magazine down and went into the treatment room. And while I sat in the chair, first waiting for the X-rays to be developed and then waiting for the novocaine to take effect, I embarked on a small, harmless-seeming daydream.

There I was, studying to be an accountant (that much was for real). I had no plans to change what seemed to be the laid-out course of my life. But accountancy, in the space of about ten minutes, had begun to look like about the dullest prospect in the world. Especially when you compared it (which is what I was doing) to the romantic, challenging, dramatic, glamorous career of a "Tracer of Missing Persons"—a Private Eye.

And the notion took hold. I left that office minus one tooth nerve, but plus one out-of-date magazine (which I'd quickly and secretly stuck under my jacket as I went out). Already, I was beginning to feel like the hero of a mystery novel.

Well, something like that, anyhow.

21   How'd You Get Into This Business, Anyway?

The magazine gave the firm's New York address, and I wrote to them, asking about a job and giving my qualifications (which, it saddened me to note, were mostly in the negative if reliable-sounding form of an unblemished citizen's record), but giving them, as well, as much of the feeling of enthusiasm as I could manage to get down on paper and into the form of a letter.

I mailed the letter, and, frankly, began to be sure I was not going to get an answer.

After all, private eyes were people you met in books or movies, weren't they? I mean, they weren't people you met in real life. . . .

The answer arrived six days later.

It came from Tracers Company of America. (The firm changed its name in 1948—I *told* you that was an out-of-date magazine—when the former title was considered too restrictive. In order not to confuse anybody, I'll use its present name from here on in, no matter what year I'm talking about.) Tracers Company said that they had sufficient representation in the state of Massachusetts, but that they were always interested in college students. So far, so good; I was a college student, all right. If that was all they needed. . . .

They'd adopted a policy, the letter told me, of allowing students to work on "missing stockholder" cases, which didn't require much in the way of specialized technique or discreet handling. Later on, of course, if anything else came along that didn't ask for too much in the way of an agent, and there was no one else to assign it to, and I happened to look right for it. . . .

The attached list contained the names of fifty

people. In all cases, their last-known addresses were twenty years old or more, and in all cases, the addresses were clustered in three small towns just west of Boston.

The letter told me that my best approach would be to research records, rather than try to track the fifty people down through direct physical means. The company told me to use my ingenuity and my imagination, and wished me luck.

Price for the job: one dollar per successful location.

Obviously, I had to do my digging without much travelling around. At rates like that, my expenses had better be kept down to zero—or, if possible, less. (I suppose that that realization marks my first professional deduction, in a way.) I checked a map—easily available, within walking distance—and noticed that all three of the towns were in the same county. That, I told myself, was going to be helpful. (Deduction number two. From then on, I quit numbering them; from then on, anyhow, I had to get down to work.)

One of my football teammates was majoring in prelaw. I asked him to ask one of his professors if there were some sort of records listing I could use for my research (as I called it), preferably records filed strictly by county.

Next morning, I had my answer: records of the probate court would be my best bet, I was told. Full of hope, and wondering if everything was going to be as easy as all that, I started out.

My first great discovery was that the probate court records had an index. That much allowed me to check out the fact that thirty-five of the fifty people on my list had died in the twenty-or-better years since they'd last been in touch with the company that had issued stock to them. Their estates had been processed through that court, and with that much information I was off and running.

The clerk was, to put it mildly, a little surprised when I submitted a requisition for thirty-five files. He calmed down a bit when I showed him my letter from Tracers Company; in fact, I was willing to bet, just then, that he'd read the same magazine article—maybe even at the same dentist's office. He gave me the files I wanted—five at a time, since that was the rule.

In each of those files, there was the name of the lawyer who represented the estate, the names of the heirs (along with their addresses as of that date, and their relationships to the people who'd left the estates), and, in some instances, even the names of the cemeteries where the burials had taken place. Back at the school dormitory that night, I went through the telephone directories for the area (still no expenses) and confirmed thirty addresses out of thirty-five.

Obviously, I was the best and the fastest private detective in the business, right then and there. Anyhow, I thought so; Tracers Company may have been a little less star struck about the matter (for one thing, that probate court idea I thought I'd invented . . . well, I found out, not too much later, that it was standard practice). But they did seem to like the results: along with payment, they sent me another batch of cases. The second batch was one hundred and fifty names long.

Before I could even start to work on them, though, I got a call from Dan Eisenberg, president of Tracers Company. He was the one, by the way, who let me in on the fact that my probate court idea was an old, old story.

Along with that deflating bit of news, though, he mentioned that he had a different sort of case, and he wondered whether I might be up to handling it. It required, he said, imagination, tact, and discretion.

Well, I thought that (for a football-playing possibly-ex-accountancy-student) I was reasonably discreet, and tactful, and even imaginative. I said as much, and he gave me the story without any trimming.

It seemed that there was a rather wealthy and socially prominent New Yorker whose only daughter was a Radcliffe student. The daughter had become infatuated, if that's the word for it, with a young man who happened to be an art instructor at Radcliffe. In fact, the daughter's letters were almost completely limited to descriptions of her plans to marry this art teacher—and the New Yorker and his wife were very thoroughly worried. They wanted to know, Mr. Eisenberg told me, whether or not the young man was "good enough" for their daughter.

(That struck me kind of funny then, and does now. I doubt if there are any two parents in the world who really think that their child's chosen mate is "good enough" or anywhere near it. Parents just don't seem to think that way.)

The decision, of course, was not going to be up to me. All I had to do was to collect facts about the instructor. Who was he? Where was he from? What had he done? What were his prospects? And so forth. The parents would take it from there.

I told Mr. Eisenberg that I would report to him in a week.

I'd grabbed the deadline out of thin air: "a week" sounded like about the right length of time. But I wasn't completely without ideas.

Radcliffe was then the "sister school" of Harvard (nowadays, as I understand it, brothers go to the sister schools and sisters go to the brother schools, thus adding to confusion, if not education). We were going to be playing against Harvard that Saturday. After the game, there'd be the usual round of dances and parties.

I kept my fingers crossed: *if* I wasn't too banged up . . . *if* I wasn't too exhausted . . . *if* something else didn't go wrong . . . I'd get to at least one of those parties, and see what I could dig up about the Radcliffe art department.

It seemed an odd sort of preoccupation for a football player. . . .

But I turned up lucky. I finished the game with no more than routine bumps and bruises. And that night, at one of the parties (oh, by the way, we won the game, in case anybody's interested; I know I was), I met a friend from high-school days. He'd gone on to Harvard and was decidedly not playing football there: it seemed he wanted to be an artist, and he was taking no chances with his hands.

Now, if I'd been a private eye in a story, I'd have spent a month or so plotting the most devious possible manner in which to find out if, just possibly, an art student at Harvard might know an art instructor at Radcliffe. But I wasn't in a story.

So I asked him.

"Sure I do," he said. "As a matter of fact, he's right over there. Want to meet him?"

Trying to look and act as nonchalant as possible, I said that I did. Of course, the whole party was pretty informal, and once we'd been introduced and we'd talked about the game a while, it wasn't very hard to shift the conversation over to the fact that I was interested in art.

True, as it happens: I'd been offered a scholarship after high school by one of the better-known art-museum schools. Sculpture, mostly.

And the art instructor, by one more cheerful coincidence, had studied at that school for a while himself. In the middle of a victory party (or, I suppose, for him, a defeat party), a thing like that was enough to make us old buddies.

Conversation got easier and easier, and finally he took me into his confidence: it seemed that *Life* magazine had just finished doing a story on the "most promising young artists in America"—a big step for recognition and reputation in anybody's book. The art instructor was going to be included in that story.

I dug up a few more facts about the guy, some at the party and some later, all without a great deal of trouble. When Monday morning rolled around, a week to the day after my talk with Mr. Eisenberg, I was talking with him again.

By the time that issue of *Life* came out, the parents of the girl involved were reassured—as far as any parents can be, ever—as to the standing and the worth of their daughter's chosen mate.

And me? I'd found a lifetime job. Tracers Company of America sent me a fifty-dollar bonus, and an invitation to spend the summer in New York City, working for them.

I took up the invitation. I've never quit.

Now, I know there are too many coincidences in this story. No writer of fiction would dare to load this many all into one small tale. My only excuse for them is that they happen to be true—and, just to make things even more uncomfortable for that fiction writer I've just invented, I'll add one more coincidence to the lot, tie off one more loose end, and make one more true statement:

I now own three paintings by that art instructor.

3
A CASE OF IDENTITY

Frankly, I just couldn't resist putting the title of a Sherlock Holmes short story at the beginning of this true story—if only because (1) it's perfectly accurate, in a very thorough sort of way, and (2) Sir Arthur Conan Doyle would spin in his grave like the working parts of a Mixmaster if he knew that his beloved Sherlock was even remotely associated with a case involving a coincidence the size of this one.

Coincidences do happen; sure. Sometimes, as in the case of the Radcliffe art instructor, you run into a whole series of them. But once in a while one comes along that even an old hand at the game doesn't quite believe—even when he knows it happened.

I'll call the man who came into my office and started all this Peter Burnett. He had a simple statement, and he made a simple request. I won't say, though, that either was—even for us—exactly in the usual course of events.

The statement: "I have six months to live."

The request: "Before I die, I'd like to find out who I am."

And, with that much for openers, I dug into the story. For him, it began in the year 1905, when he was three and a half years old.

In that year his mother died. Her name hadn't been Burnett; neither had his father's. At three and a half, "Peter Burnett" had been known, to family and the few friends one tends to have at that age, as David Opperman.

Wilhelm Opperman, his father, had suddenly and unexpectedly been left with six children, including David; and taking care of six children, plus handling a job to make the money so that he could *afford* to take care of them, just did not seem possible. He couldn't go up against the impossible. He went up, instead, against the unbelievably difficult—and made what seemed to him then both a fantastically painful and an absolutely necessary decision. The children had to be brought up properly, in proper homes; they had to have enough food and clothing to go on with; and Wilhelm Opperman saw no way of providing that. So he provided the six with other homes.

They were the homes of friends—homes in which, as he was able to assure himself, each child would have not only a mother and a father, not only a financially sound upbringing, but some love, some caring, some sense of belonging.

Then he did what he had to do: he disappeared. There are a lot of heroes who never get mentioned in the history books.

At any rate: David was given to Joseph and Mary Burnett, who renamed him Peter. As it happened, the Burnetts moved out of the neighborhood within a short time. Peter (as I'll call him most of the way from here on) never saw his father or his brothers and sisters again.

Being very young, his memory dimmed rapidly: he was Peter Burnett. And with that he became contented. If his brief Opperman childhood ever returned to him, it must have done so in the form of dreams or vague reveries, hardly worth mentioning and certainly not worth remembering.

He was Peter Burnett, and Peter Burnett had an interesting and a busy life. He was in the service during World War I as a machinist in the Navy. After his discharge, he worked hard and steadily at his trade, advancing as the years went on and becoming, as his work began to pay off for him, a highly skilled workman.

He was at the edge of that position, and knew it, when (in 1928) he married. The marriage was a happy one, even though the Burnett couple, after consulting with doctors, discovered that they could never have children of their own. They had each other, and it seemed to both of them to be enough.

His work continued; his marriage continued; and between 1928 and 1942 there's not much about Peter Burnett's career that's very different—given a change in years, say—from your career. Or mine.

In 1942 he had a determined future ahead of him; that much was certain. His reputation as a skilled workman was growing, and his home was very much worth coming home to. He thought, too, that he had a solid and an understandable past behind him—but in that year the proof that he was wrong began to turn up.

Mary Burnett died.

Before she did, she had Peter called to her. She had to pull a string or two, because he was by then back in the Navy. Overage or not, he'd enlisted, thinking that his experience would at least make up for the age difference. Apparently Mary Burnett had the strings to pull, because Peter was given leave to see the woman he thought of as his mother.

And of course, from her deathbed, Mary Burnett told him the truth; and Peter's past dissolved.

She told him that she was not his natural mother. She told him what had happened thirty-seven years before. She told him that he had three brothers and two sisters, and she told him their names.

That was that. She didn't have any more information.

Peter had, very suddenly, a basket of facts with which, it seemed, he could do nothing at all.

He'd lived such a normal, happy life. . . up to then

At first he was filled with frantic resentment against his father. After all, he told himself, the old man had cared so little for him that he'd just given him away, along with the other five. Resentment was easy to feel; to some extent, and for a little while, it filled the hole that Peter had suddenly found opening up in his life.
But then. . . .
Back on duty, aboard ship, he began to think things through a little more carefully. He began to see that what his father—his real father—had done might very well have been an expression, not of indifference, but of the deepest sort of love. Perhaps (at first, just perhaps, and no more)—perhaps his father had really, deeply, sincerely, loved him after all.
And perhaps he had loved the other five—his brothers and sisters, whom he couldn't even remember—just as well.
Perhaps. . . .
All right: but the middle of the Pacific, in the middle of a war, is no place to begin a hunt for missing persons (anyhow, it hasn't been so far; any day now, I may learn something new). Peter could do nothing but wonder, and wait . . . and wonder, and wait again . . . all the while keeping up with his work as a machinist aboard ship. He began to have new dreams, different ones . . . dreams that weren't very pleasant. . . .
Whereupon Japan took the first step toward solving his problem for him. By trying to kill him, of course.
The kamikaze pilot sank his ship and nearly killed

him right there and then. (One other person actually *was* killed—but we'll get to him, I'm afraid, a bit later in the story.)

Peter remembered being thrown screaming into the water, surrounded by wreckage and by burning oil, hearing the screams of other men he couldn't even get to . . . seeing the lifeless forms that still floated. He even remembered, more or less, losing consciousness.

From that point on things were hazy, and continued hazy for some while. He awoke, in a world of unbearable pain, and he was aboard a hospital ship bound for Pearl Harbor. He awoke again, and again. The pain didn't go away, though it rose and fell a little; that was his world, and all his world.

From Pearl Harbor he was taken to a hospital in the U.S. It was fine being back in the States, but the pain kept attacking him, and he kept blacking out again. And again. And. . . .

There were operations. He remembered some of the things about them, and he didn't much want to remember a lot more. Not one operation, but an endless series, while the pain never let go, while the haze surrounded him . . . sometimes he could hear his voice and he couldn't tell if it were saying anything.

Or screaming. . . .

And slowly he came back to the world. The world had pain in it, but it had other things too. It had a hospital room, a bed, a nurse. . . .

And a doctor, who told him that there were to be no more operations. "Nothing will improve matters much further." He could hear that, all right, and even understand it. He could do quite a lot: he could walk and talk, see and hear; but he couldn't go on living. Not for very much more.

Nothing any doctor in any hospital could do would arrest the steady, speedy, march of death on his broken body. The kamikaze pilot had had his success . . . at long distance.

He was an outpatient then; he could travel. He came to Tracers Company with that six-month sentence hanging like a sword over his head, ringing like a constant bell in his ears.

There was no time. Not any more. What he wanted done, he had to get done—before the doctors told him— before he knew, for himself—that it was too late.

"I'd like to find out who I am," he said. And I knew we had an urgent case.

We needed facts, and Peter Burnett had the facts for us. He knew that his father, Wilhelm Opperman, and his mother, Sarah, had lived at 451 Morton Street in Dorchester, Massachusetts. He knew that Sarah had died in that building, on November 19, 1905. (Don't bother checking out all these numbers. They aren't real. Nor are the names involved. These people deserve their own life; they'll have it.)

Coincidence popped up for the first—but not the last—time in the case. I hate to argue with the mystery story writers, but coincidence *does* pop up, more often than you'd think. This one:

In an odd sort of way, Peter and I were distant

neighbors. Dorchester is a suburb of Boston, and so is Worcester, where I grew up and where my mother still has a pot of chicken soup on the stove "just in case" I happen to stop in. The distance between the two suburbs is about forty miles, and I can still remember the basketball games and the cheering, maybe twice a year . . . Worcester Community Center vs. Dorchester Community Center.

The big game. And, in those years, it was. It was. Maybe, for the kids growing up around there now, it still is (but I doubt it). . . .

The games, and the dances that followed them. . . .

Years before my own memories, had Peter Burnett (or his brothers, his sisters) gone to those games, danced at those dances, cheered and laughed and imagined that the world was simple, that the world made sense?

It was a sentimental way to be thinking, for a man on a job. After all, nobody at 451 Morton Street remembered the dances now. No one remembered the Opperman family; no one remembered the Burnetts, who had taken David Opperman into their home, and had done the best they knew how to do, trying to fulfill the wishes of a helpless father.

So the work began. No matter what you think or what you feel, the work is the same; there are routines, there are obvious places to check, obvious moves to make.

The Boston City Directory, for instance.

Dorchester is a suburb made up of rows of respectable three-family houses, inhabited (in those years) mostly by immigrants from Europe. The directory had their names, most of them, and I began to track the immigrants down, one by one, hoping that someone would remember.

But the immigrants were gone. The past was hard to recall. The past had been lost in the shadows of those houses, between the words of an old man, under the cement of the worn familiar sidewalks. . . . "Ever hear of a family named Opperman? Used to live at 451?"

"Ever hear of. . . ."

No.

No.

It was the sort of case you give up on, not because it can't be solved but because, the way things shape up, there just isn't enough money to pay for the time you'd have to spend solving it. You check everything you can think of, as well as you can, for as long as financially possible . . . and then you let it go. You've got a living to make; you have to let it go.

But this case wasn't one I was going to give up on easily. All I had was one question, which isn't much in the way of ammunition. I asked it of everyone I could find, and I went on asking. . . .

Until, at last, I met the little old lady who ran the candy store on the corner. I went in and I ordered a Coke and I almost didn't ask the question at all, I was so afraid of one more no. But:

"Ever hear of a family named Opperman? Used to live—"

She stopped me. Looking as if she'd have liked to be friendly, but you never know: I might be a bill collector. Or worse. "Oppie?" she said, and I nodded.

"Why—Oppie, he stayed around here as long as he could, that one. Just as long . . . retired last year, you know. Last year, that's all: retired, and moved to Florida." The pause, and the suspicious blink; you learn to expect that, and not wonder about it or react to it. "Why? You a friend of his?"

Coincidences happen, and I was afraid this was going to be one. The rug was going to be pulled out from under me and I was going to be left with nothing more than a hoarse voice and my single question, over and over and over again . . . but: "I think we've got friends in common," I said, and, very quietly and very slowly, I asked a few more questions. About the Oppermans; about the Burnetts. For the man who was a son of both families.

But it was no coincidence. "Oppie," it turned out rapidly enough, was Max Opperman, the eldest of the six children. The family that had taken him in hadn't changed his name; he was far too old for that— eleven, going on twelve.

And, being older, he'd managed to keep in touch with all of the others—all of them, that is, except David. The little old lady explained it to me: "The story is, little Davey died a long time ago. Anyhow . . . Oppie named his youngest after Davey. And now this new Davey—now he's dead, too."

The namesake was dead; but the original, as I knew, was alive.

And from there on, the job was easy.

Max Opperman had taken to running "Oppie's Cabins," down off Route 1 and north of Hollywood, Florida—he was simple enough to trace. In fact, about all the time the job took, from there on, was the time required to get down there and to tell him that his brother David was alive, and looking for him.

"If only Papa could know . . . ," Max began—and then took a deep breath and started making plans. He knew where to find the rest of the family, of course, and he got in touch with them, and then with "Peter Burnett" back in New York.

He set up a full family reunion—the first since 1905.

In fact, the Oppermans invited me to that party, and I can't remember having a better time.

It was about a month later that I got a call from my client—wanting, he said, to thank me and to fill me in on a few family details. Of course, I knew his voice as soon as he said hello, and I said:

"Peter—"

"No," he said. "Dave. David Opperman."

Coincidences?

They happen. When you swear you wouldn't have believed it . . . when it's a one-in-a-million chance.

They happen.

The namesake—young David Opperman (it was "Oppie" who told me, by the way)—had died in the same kamikaze attack that had injured his uncle.

He'd been on the same ship. Hurt, he'd been

picked up by the same ship, and taken to the same Pearl Harbor hospital.

And there, he had died—while his uncle, presumed dead years before, had lived, and had recovered enough to make his search, and complete it . . . well within his own dark time limit.

4
AS SANE AS I AM

Some of the best actors I have ever seen were not doing their performing in front of movie or TV cameras, or before a live audience on or off Broadway. They have been people who were convinced (or at least fervently *wanting* to be convinced) that what they were acting out was the truth.

A case in point:

Nina Haslett had been travelling aboard the Orange Blossom Special from Miami to New York. She had said goodnight to her sister-in-law, Madge Haslett, in the club car about 9:00 P.M. At breakfast time the next morning, Madge discovered that Nina was gone. There was no indication of where along the line she had left the train.

Later that day, Nina Haslett's two brothers, Glen and Roger, came to my office. They seemed embarrassed over the whole situation, and I couldn't understand why. It did occur to me, though, that they were concerned with something more than just the fact that their sister was missing.

They told me that, as near as they could figure, Nina had gotten off the train somewhere north of Charleston and south of Baltimore. I asked whether they had notified the railroad—she might have met with an accident. They said they had not. They knew she had gotten off deliberately.

I asked how they knew, and they said she was a mental case.

I was told that Nina Haslett had suffered two nervous breakdowns in the previous three years. Following the second one, her sister-in-law had taken her to Miami for a rest. It hadn't helped much. In fact, Nina had seemed to get worse. Twice, she had tried to run away. After the second try, phone consultation between the psychiatrist in New York and the one in Miami resulted in the tentative diagnosis of Nina as a manic-depressive. Informed of this, the brothers urged Madge to bring Nina home. When Madge found out that Nina was gone, she got off the train (at Baltimore) and called New York. Her husband told her to check into a hotel and wait for further word.

That night, I caught a plane for Baltimore and, in less than two hours, I met with Madge Haslett at the hotel bar.

Madge ran through the story for me. She told me how she had tried to keep Nina in sight at all times . . . even how she had tried to stay awake most nights. But that last week in Florida had been too much. That had been when she'd decided to call her husband in New York. And he'd told her to come on back with Nina.

I had picked up a timetable for the Orange Blossom Special, and learned that the train made five stops between 9:00 P.M. and 9:00 A.M. I told Madge that we would have to squeeze it down. "It could have been any one of them," she said. "I didn't see her all night."

"Did she have much money with her?" I asked.

"No cash," said Madge, "I wouldn't let her have any. She may have her check book with her, but that's all. I even kept her luggage in my compartment. It's over there. I had it brought down."

There were a couple of bags and a coat in a corner. "Is this all of it?" I asked.

"Yes, except for a vanity case," said Madge.

"Funny, she took the case but not the coat."

"She had a raincoat, too," said Madge. "It's a red satin one, with a hood."

There it was . . . a possible way of determining where Nina had gotten off the train. "Do you remember if it rained anywhere along the line?" I asked Madge.

"No," she answered, "but maybe it did while I was asleep."

I asked one final question. "Can you think of any friends she might go to?"

"No, not in that part of the country," said Madge. "Do you think you can find her?"

"We usually do . . . sooner or later."

"I think it had better be sooner," Madge told me, sort of under her breath.

"What do you mean?" I said.

"She's a very sick girl . . . despondent . . . I'm afraid what the doctor said might come true. She might try to kill herself."

I requested the railroad to give me the weather conditions for the previous night at all five stops. I told them they could wire the information to me aboard the train, and I headed for the station.

Nina had no money with her. It was possible she might have been able to cash a check somewhere. (Madge Haslett told me that Nina had over one hundred thousand dollars in a bank in New York. It was her share of an inheritance that had been split three ways with her brothers.) I sat alone and mulled over the possibilities of solving this case before it was too late . . . and my reverie was interrupted by the conductor tapping me on the shoulder. "Word just came in," he said. "The company checked all the stations between Baltimore and Charleston. It was raining last night only in one place: Norfolk, Virginia."

Within an hour, I was in the stationmaster's office at Norfolk. He told me that the Orange Blossom Special, heading north, pulls into the station at 12:52 A.M. and leaves at 1:17 A.M. It had been right on time the previous night.

I asked him where someone could cash a check at

that hour. He said he didn't think anyone could cash a check there at any hour. The only place open was his office and the coffee counter. I asked him if he'd been on duty the previous night.

When he said yes, I showed him the picture of Nina Haslett that her brothers had given me in New York. He said she looked familiar.

"Police trouble?" he asked.

"No," I told him. "She's a mental patient."

"Who says so?"

"Her family," I said.

He hesitated a moment and then: "I talked with her last night," he confessed. "She didn't have a cent in her purse. Sure, I cashed a check for her. Ten bucks. I'd do it again. So would you," he finished, a bit defiantly.

"I would?" I said, "What makes you think so"?

"Nice a girl as you would ever want to meet. But—something funny going on here, mister," he continued.

"What do you mean?"

"Well," he went on, "a stationmaster gets to meet a lot of people and he gets to know all the different types. I'll tell you one thing. Nothing wrong with that girl. As sane as I am."

The stationmaster assured me that he was right about the girl. He told me he had cashed the check out of his own pocket. She said she'd needed it for cab fare to a hotel. She had asked him to recommend one. He had. It was the Surf Hotel.

I called the Surf Hotel. Nina Haslett was registered there. She had left word at the desk that she was not to be disturbed—unless the call were from a man named

Daniel Bradford.

So, I hopped into a cab and gave the address of the hotel. I crossed the lobby and asked the desk clerk what room Miss Haslett was in.

"Are you Daniel Bradford?" he asked.

"No."

"Oh." A medium-size pause. "Well, Miss Haslett checked out about ten minutes ago."

I asked if she had left a forwarding address . . . and I probably would have done a real double take if he said yes. That didn't happen. The next best thing did.

"No, she didn't," he said, "but she'll be calling in later for messages. She's expecting to hear from Mr. Bradford."

"It's important that I reach her," I said, "Did she say where she was going?"

"Well," said the desk clerk, "she did ask directions to Hampton Roads. That's where the Naval Air Station is."

I asked for, and got, the same directions. He asked whether I would like to leave a message for when Miss Haslett called. I told him I would. . . . "Tell her that Mr. Bradford will meet her here at four o'clock."

And I headed for the ferry, a thought running through my mind: sure, Nina Haslett was acting rationally; her impression on the stationmaster and the desk clerk confirmed that.

But if Madge Haslett's fears had any basis at all, a boat was the one place Nina should not be.

The chances of overtaking her were remote at best. But I had to try.

It was clear I had missed the ferry that Nina had taken. The one I boarded was just about ready to take on passengers as I got to it.

As we crossed the water, I did a little rail leaning . . . and then, one of those crazy time-stopping moments happened. As I watched the ferry making the return trip pass us on the starbaord side, I saw another rail-leaner on the other boat.

No mistaking it.

Red satin raincoat, with a hood. It was Nina Haslett.

I started to shout to her, but restrained myself. No telling what she would do, if she could hear me, I thought, but I doubted she could hear me anyhow.

My fantasy mind did a little overtime, conjuring up ways to board that passing boat. Just fantasy, though: no sense.

An hour later, I was on my way back to Norfolk.

(People follow patterns. As I have mentioned before, it is the familiarity with those patterns that enables the experienced searcher to predict the movements and activities of his quarry. But things just didn't seem to be fitting in here. I was beginning to conclude that Nina Haslett was that rare case: the unpredictable runaway. Of course, this case would be one where time was of the essence: there was no margin for being wrong.)

There was no way to guess where she had gone after returning to Norfolk, but it was a certainty that she would get around to realizing that her family would attempt to find her. I had to locate her before she left the city.

I had one chance. If she phoned the hotel for her messages, she might go back there to meet Daniel Bradford—whoever he was.

I got to the Surf Hotel at 3:10 P.M. I asked if there was a house doctor and the desk clerk rang his number and connected me with him. I told him the story in about thirty seconds but the doctor wanted to know a lot more than that a young woman had run away and was staying at the hotel. I told him that she was described as a manic-depressive, with suicidal tendencies. He wished me luck, and told me that, if I did find her, I'd better be very alert. He told me to keep a close eye on her. "If she's very depressed, she might try to do herself in." Then he added the punch line: "If she goes the other way, watch out."

"What do you mean?" I asked.

"She might turn on you," he said . . . and he hung up.

I took a seat in the lobby, in a spot where I could keep the desk in sight, while I read the local newspaper.

Four o'clock came and went. So did 4:15 and 4:30. I had gotten all the way down to the crossword puzzle. (These days, I spend as little time as possible on the news, considering what it consists of.)

A voice said, "I'm Nina Haslett. Are you a friend of Danny's?"

"No, I'm not."

"Then," she said, "I suppose you're a detective.

Did Madge send you?" She seemed to laugh almost. "You must be awfully efficient. How did you find me so fast?"

"Sorry. Trade secret."

"Well, now that you've found me, what are you going to do?"

"Let's go someplace and talk it over."

"We can go up to my room, if you'd like." She saw me hesitate. "Does that frighten you?"

"No, should it?"

"Of course! Didn't they tell you about me?"

"A little."

"Then you know . . . I'm supposed to be crazy."

Nina Haslett gave a musical little laugh, as though she hadn't a trouble in the world. The stationmaster was right . . . this was a nice girl. The question was: what else was she?

We entered her room. (I thought that desk clerk said she had checked out.) She was relaxed and seemingly very happy. There were several boxes on the bed, obviously containing new clothes she had bought earlier in the day.

"I suppose my brothers are furious at Madge for letting me get away," she said. "It really wasn't her fault, though. She's just an immoral woman."

I asked what she meant by that.

She told me that Madge had gotten acquainted with a man in the club car. It couldn't have worked out better. It gave Nina a chance to get off the train at Norfolk, right where she wanted to.

"Why here?" I asked.

"Well, to meet Danny, of course," she told me. "He's stationed over at Hampton Roads now. They didn't know that, you see. They thought he was still out on the West Coast. We're getting married tomorrow."

Then she went on to explain that she was determined to marry Daniel Bradford, Lieutenant, jg, U.S. Navy. She knew that her brothers disapproved. But not for the usual reasons (you know, not good enough, etc.). What she told me was that her brothers wanted control over her money—the money she had inherited. Her brothers had gone into business together, she explained, and were losing their shirts. They needed her money to bail themselves out. So, they had simply decided to have her certified insane so she'd be out of their way.

"Where's your fiancé now?" I asked.

"At the Navy base," she told me. "He'll be on duty until tomorrow. I went over to see him but I couldn't."

"Are you going to wait here for him?"

"That depends on you—doesn't it?"

"I can't *drag* you back to your family."

"If you tell them where I am, they'll come for me."

"That's what I was hired for."

"But if you wait, Danny and I will be safely married before they get here. You can watch me; you can sleep right outside my door."

Now I was *really* undecided about this whole setup. I had heard both sides of this story. Someone was making things up here, and I simply didn't know who. I wanted a little time.

I told Nina that she needn't fear my taking any immediate action, and I made a date to meet her in the hotel dining room in twenty minutes. We would talk more over dinner.

I called my office from the booth in the lobby and instructed one of the investigators there to get in touch with Glen Haslett and check out Nina's story. I told him to wire me that evening in care of the hotel physician. Meanwhile, he was to assure the Hasletts that I wouldn't let Nina out of my sight.

More than twenty-five minutes passed. I was beginning to get worried . . . thinking about either calling Nina's room or going right on up there . . . when she stepped out of the elevator.

She read my face: "Worried?" she said. "You shouldn't have been. You know that when a woman says twenty minutes, she means at least a half hour."

We sat down to a pleasant dinner, and I must say I admired her restraint. Finally, though, she couldn't hold it back any longer. "You haven't told me yet," she said. "Is there going to be a wedding tomorrow?"

"Well," I assured her, "I didn't wire your brothers yet."

With that, she invited me to the wedding.

And I accepted.

I paid the dinner check and, just as we were leaving the dining room, the hotel doctor appeared at the door. He handed me the telegram he had just received from New York. Nina asked me who he was. I told her he was just an employee of the hotel.

"You're lying," she said. "He's a doctor."

"How can you tell?" I asked.

"I can always tell," she said, getting really worked up by then. "You've had him spying on me all night! You thought I didn't know. You thought you had me fooled!"

"Maybe it was the other way around," I said, as mildly as possible.

By that time, she was screaming a lot of unintelligible things and, frankly, I was relieved to see the doctor go to her and soothingly ask her to step into his office. Of course, she went—along with him, happy to get away from me . . . her betrayer. They disappeared into the doctor's office.

I opened the telegram. It read: "Lt. Daniel Bradford killed four years ago in a plane crash. San Diego Naval Base. Psychiatrist says Nina Haslett unquestionably deranged."

The shock of her fiancé's death had been simply too much for Nina Haslett to bear. She had continued to search for him and, as long as she was able to pretend that he was alive, she took on the appearance and demeanor of a normal, healthy and very attractive woman.

The last I heard, by the way, she was in a sanitarium and making good progress.

The pursuit of this investigation taught me something about truth. I learned that truth, to twist a phrase, is very often in the mind of the pretender.

INTERLUDE I

When I was studying to be an accountant, I had a trench coat.
    I don't now.

    If you want to disappear, make sure that no one either loves you or hates you enough to make a real search for you. If the hunt isn't called off—you'll be found.

    People who have inferiority complexes are usually

right—and inferior.

Once, when I was trailing a person who was expected to give me a lead to someone else I was looking for, the person I was trailing grabbed the only taxi in sight—the sort of occupational hazard you're supposed to make sure never happens. It almost never does.

I looked up and down the street for another cab. The cab I'd missed blew his horn at one cruising by, and it stopped and picked me up. I gave him: "Follow that cab," and he asked me: "Which one?"

"The one that just stopped you for me."

If a private detective looked like a private detective—he couldn't get a job as a private detective.

I wouldn't know Judge Crater if he stepped on my foot.

I get at least a hundred letters a year from people who claim to be part owners of the land on which the city of Baltimore now stands. This is part of the oldest con game originated in the U.S., but it goes on fooling people every year, and the number per year doesn't change much, no matter what. I wish I knew why.

Interlude I

The qualities people dislike in other people are—dependably—the qualities they have themselves. The more dislike, the stronger the quality.

5
THE
FINISH LINE

It doesn't happen often, obviously. Most of the cases we handle are jobs no one else is at work on. Nobody hires six agencies to find a missing husband (anyhow, not six agencies all at the same time) or to check on a reputation.

But every once in a while there's a race for information. The setup has to involve, of course, more than one interested party—and, hence, more than one agency; and, usually, matters work out so that everyone starts at about the same time, with about the same amount of information. It's a little like one of those TV game shows—or maybe a horse race.

And it isn't much smarter to bet on the results of one of these chases than it is to bet, blind and at random, on the average horse race. Hard work, expertise, intuition all have their place, sure—but at the finish line you may still be beaten (or end up the winner yourself) on nothing more than a single bit of luck you were quick enough to take the right advantage of.

I remember one of those chases vividly: it involved the mineral rights covering oil land, and—naturally—it all began with a phone call from Texas.

Whenever my secretary tells me that a man from Texas is on the line, I get just about the same picture: a combination of John Wayne movies and *Giant*. There's this big, open country—the hard-bitten, rough-hewn man going home (after a hard day's work punching cattle or mebbe whuppin' the tarnation outen rustlers) to a baronial mansion complete with eight or nine (or fifteen or sixty-seven) big cars parked in the garages and around the enormous circular driveway—the pack of hunting dogs galloping on the acres of lawn. . . .

Oh, sure, I know perfectly well that there are a few Texans who don't live that way . . . but I can't get the picture out of my head. And the call that came in that day was from the secretary of a man who began to sound, in the brief sketch she gave me of the problem and his dealings with it, very much like the picture, at that.

He was en route to New York by private plane, you see, and in radio contact with his offices in Texas; and he'd instructed his secretary to arrange an appointment with me for that afternoon.

In fact, the picture not only grew stronger, it grew stranger as well. I kept trying to imagine the plane landing on the roof of 515 Madison Avenue, and the Texan (roughhewn, hard-bitten) uncoiling his lasso, hitching it to a bit of cornice or some such, and coming down hand over hand to our eleventh-floor offices.

It wasn't a picture that made any sense at all. But for three hours it interfered with any other things I was trying to do. I suppose Texas just gets to me, somehow. . . .

At the end of three hours, he walked in, accompanied by his lawyer and looking just like a normal non-Texan human being, and we began a full-dress and somewhat complicated conference. A great deal of background detail went into the eventual asking of one small question—and, as I keep finding out, it's those "one small question" jobs that turn out to be the killers. This one wasn't even close to being an exception.

Background, then, first:

Oil had been discovered, very recently, about fifty miles north of Columbus, Ohio. There was a lot of oil land in Ohio, and that much was no surprise, but production had shrunk to nearly nothing, until some wildcatters came in and drilled a well into a spot in Morrow County. At three thousand two hundred and eighty feet they hit a gusher; two more gushers came in almost at once; and, within a shorter time than it takes to count the money involved in a deal like that, four hundred and fifty wells had been dug. Of those, one hundred and sixty-two turned out to be producers—which is a good deal better average than an oilman figures on.

Buying drilling rights, and bidding on tracts of land, of course, began at once. One particularly wild case involved a bid up from one dollar an acre to thirty thousand dollars an acre inside of a single day. Rigs, derricks, tools, setups appeared on front lawns and in back alleys, displacing vegetable gardens, taking over back yards.

Except...

One hundred years before, the right-of-way across a corner of a piece of Morrow County property had been granted, by the farmer who owned the land, to the railroad company that wanted to run a spur line through. The right-of-way, naturally, applied to surface rights and nothing more; the mineral rights remained the farmer's property. No one ever really doubted that he'd lost track of such rights; they were worth nothing in particular at the time. But nobody doubted, either, that his descendants didn't even know about the ownership.

Those descendants, whoever they were, owned the mineral rights to the strip of land. As for me . . . well, "It's a nice, simple job," I was told.

After a while, in my business, you get to hate the sound of those words.

"All you have to do," the Texan went on, "is to find the descendants, and put me in touch with them."

Sure.

There was only one additional fact. We weren't the

only people who knew about the strip of land, by any means. And everybody who thought he might want to bid on the mineral rights was looking for those same descendants.

It wasn't exactly what you'd call a lonely job.

In fact, there were times when it reminded me, not of Texas, but of a somewhat nearer vision: New York's rush-hour traffic.

Complete with money.

The Texan had given me a check, and had told me, with admirable casualness of tone, to "get in touch at any time—my office will know where to reach me, even if I'm in my plane."

Great.

There wasn't, after a full description of the "nice, simple job," a lot more to discuss, so, the next morning, Bob Eisenberg (our chief investigator in the New York area) and I went out to Columbus, Ohio by plain old commercial plane. We picked up a rented car at the airport, and we started north, toward Morrow County.

Ten miles before we crossed the county line, we started noticing No Vacancy signs on the motels. By the time we were at the county seat, a town called Mt. Gilead, we had begun to get some idea of the size of the excitement this new oil rush had stirred up.

It seemed as if fifty thousand people were trying to get into the office of the county clerk—to check registers, wills, anything else that might offer the faintest hint of a clue—all at once, and every one of them with sharp elbows, and the whole fifty thousand talking at once at the top of one hundred thousand collective lungs.

One long look was enough. Maybe, Bob and I thought, just maybe there was a side door into the problem—a side door without so many elbows or so many screaming voices.

Clearly, trying to get anything whatever out of the chaos surrounding the county clerk was going to take days, if not years. But (it occurred to us) trying to get something out of the county historical society, now . . . that was a different matter. Nobody, it seemed, had thought of that one—obviously, they must have been telling each other, if everybody was heading for the county clerk, then the county clerk must be the place to go.

Unfortunately for all the people who restfully trusted the wits of the crowd instead of whatever their own minds might have told them if they'd stopped long enough to listen, the information was where nobody had looked for it: in the historical society's records.

Mt. Gilead, we learned, hadn't always been in Morrow County at all. It had been in Marion County, just to the west; and the records there (where things weren't in the least crowded, or confused) began to throw information into our hunt just as soon as we started to consult them.

(For some strange reason—carelessness, probably—we didn't bother to inform the other hunters that they were searching the wrong field. Must have been carelessness. I can't imagine another reason.)

So:

A deed was conveyed on the property in question (the Marion County Clerk's Office informed us) to one Jonas Bailey, on March 12, 1827. I got on the wire to New York and asked our research people back there to check out the federal census for 1850, 1860 and 1870 for that name—and to get back to me, in a nice, peaceful, uncrowded Marion County motel, by morning.

But we weren't through, by any means.

Marion County had a historical society, too—and, on the twin principles that any information at all may turn out helpful, and that what works once may just decide to work twice, we went over to dig through its records.

It was Bob who found the notation that mentioned Jonas Bailey. He'd been the first "Exhorter" of the M. E. Church in Mt. Gilead. "Exhorter" was a licensed position; Bailey had held it until 1864.

The same note added that, before the church had been erected, the meetings has been held at the Bailey home.

Clearly, our next stop ought to have been where the church records might be kept. That (the historical society librarian told us) was about fifteen miles away, in Delaware, Ohio, at Ohio Wesleyan University—right on back toward Columbus. All right; we'd stop there on the way back. Meanwhile, though, we might get something out of a visit to the Methodist church that existed, still, right in Mt. Gilead itself.

I didn't expect much, due to the operation of a natural law which states that all churches burn down three months to three years before you need to consult their records. It's a law I have never known to fail, and the Mt. Gilead case provided no exception: the original building had long ago gone up in smoke.

The new pastor (he'd been on the job for six months) had never heard of a Bailey family; neither had his secretary. And Bob and I walked slowly and sadly out of that pastoral office, at the rear of the church. We headed down the center aisle toward the front entrance and our car outside.

And what happened next is, I'm afraid, going to sound completely nutty.

As we walked down that center aisle, the late-afternoon sun glinted off a metal plaque underneath the big stained-glass window over the front doors. The glint drew my eye to the plaque.

It read: IN MEMORY OF JONAS BAILEY AND SAMUEL GILMAN—ELIZABETH B. GILMAN.

I looked at Bob. He'd caught the plaque, too; that little stab of sunlight had told us very nearly all we wanted to know.

Clearly, Elizabeth B(ailey) had married a man named Gilman. Jonas Bailey had been her father; Samuel Gilman was either husband or father-in-law.

It seemed obvious, and unbelievably easy. But we couldn't check any of it out then: the various records offices and the probate court had closed for the day.

"Tomorrow," I said, and we went on back to our peaceful motel and checked with New York. After that, there wasn't any need to check out that Ohio Wesleyan church; the office had done a fast job, and the checkout was just beautiful to see.

    The 1850 census:
        Jonas Bailey, born 1795
        Penelope Bailey, his wife, born 1800
        William, a son, born 1823
        Elijah, a son, born 1825
        Elizabeth, a daughter, born 1830.
    The 1860 census:
        Jonas Bailey
        Penelope Bailey.
    The 1870 census:
        Nobody.

So: between 1850 and 1860 the two sons, had married and moved away, or just moved away, or died, leaving the daughter as the easiest surviving relative to check out. She'd married a man named Gilman (Benjamin, it turned out; Samuel was the father-in-law). The probate court had the records of her estate.

Her husband had died before her; they'd had no children.

And that left the brothers William and Elijah, and their children—with addresses, as easy to turn up as any I can remember, in Idaho, Michigan, Indiana and California.

By the time we'd finished the complete job, I began to think that our Texas client had some real use for that plane. There were thirty-two living great-grandchildren of Jonas Bailey scattered all over the United States, including one in the Virgin Islands.

We'd documented every one of those thirty-two as a legitimate heir of Jonas Bailey, and a part owner of that strip of land's mineral rights. The rest of the job belonged to our Texan.

Afterthought No.1: The Texan. I couldn't resist checking back with him, some time later, and he told me there was no doubt in the world there was a gusher under those railroad tracks. In fact, I understand it's gushing right now.

Afterthought No. 2: Well . . . nowadays, my image of a Texan has changed—slightly. Now, I think of him as a hot-rod jet pilot.

6
THE ENTIRELY MISSING PERSON

I suppose the case of Donna Linfoot was, all in all, the single strangest case we've ever handled. Tracers Company was hired to identify a young woman, with the proviso that if our hunt showed up the faintest possibility of the woman's having committed a crime we were to stop work instantly. A good part of the background with which we started was the report of a recurrent dream. And we had absolutely no idea who our client was.

She gave her name as Donna Linfoot, and when she came into my office she said she was a missing person. "About as missing as you can be," she said. "You see, I have no idea who I am."

I said something like: "What?" and she went on, hesitantly:

"I—it's amnesia. I just don't know—I haven't any idea who I am. I read about you people in a magazine, and I—thought maybe you could help me."

True amnesia is much rarer than any TV viewer might imagine. The girl in my office was young, pretty, and carried no visible marks of the blow on the head or the physical collapse that sometimes causes temporary amnesia. I must have looked a little doubtful.

"You've got to help me," she said. "There isn't anyone else."

I started to say: "The police—"

She stopped me right there. "No. This has to be confidential." She shut her eyes for a second and then slowly opened them again. "You see—I think I may have murdered someone."

Frankly, the situation at that point looked so much like a TV show that I began to think I was the victim of someone's motiveless put-on. Once in a while, I suppose, life imitates art; Donna Linfoot's story was no joke. She was entirely serious, and entirely terrified.

It didn't take long for her to give me the background. She was working as a secretary in Washington, D. C. She'd applied for a secretarial job she'd seen in the want ads, and as far as she could judge she'd been doing the same sort of work before her own special "black curtain," as one writer has called the barrier of amnesia, descended. She had arrived in Washington on a bus, but she had no idea where she'd got on that bus: the curtain had come down somewhere en route—at a "rest stop" thirty minutes long, three hours away from Washington, she had awakened from a nightmare, left the bus to freshen herself up and shake off the cobwebs of her dream, and looked into a mirror.

She had seen an absolute stranger.

She remembered nothing before that moment, except the dream. She was very clear on the dream: she'd been having it, every few nights, ever since. It had, she told me, very little real continuity; the main element in it was a gun. The gun went off and killed someone— someone who seemed, in the dream, clear and familiar but who faded immediately when Donna awoke, and could not be remembered or identified.

She also discovered, she continued, that she had an absolute and inexplicable terror of policemen—of men in any uniform that resembled police clothing.

I asked about her name. She'd picked it, she said, for no particular reason; the name "Donna Linfoot" had just occurred to her.

I suggested the police, and then what seemed a better and more natural possibility: a psychiatrist. But Donna was terrified at the thought. She felt she could trust no one except Tracers Company to follow her strict instructions and keep matters confidential. It was a great compliment—but it was, too, a frighteningly demanding job.

The only thing worse than taking on that job and failing—which was a possibility I had to consider—was refusing to take it on at all.

So I went to Washington.

Donna Linfoot's apartment showed me no trace of her character or her past—or of anyone's. There was nothing in the apartment itself to take me a step further. I asked Donna about the various personal belongings put neatly in place there, and wasn't surprised when she told me she'd bought them since arriving in Washington.

She hadn't had anything when she arrived—no luggage, not even a purse. She had been carrying thirty dollars, she said, in her coat pocket.

So I took a look at the coat, though she was sure it would tell me nothing; there had, after all, been nothing else in the pockets. She'd looked.

But I wasn't checking the pockets; I wanted a look at the label. And there was one: *Hess Brothers, Allentown, Pa.* The name rang no bell.

She had a couple of packs of matches, too. They came from Pittsburgh and Harrisburg, both in Pennsylvania. No city or state name rang a bell with her. She offered the notion that the bus, in getting to Washington, had stopped at all those places, but a quick look at a map knocked that idea out. It would have meant traveling in a circle; whatever route the bus had taken, it wouldn't have looked like that.

Donna took the matches, and I went on to Allentown—which wasn't very helpful. The coat, according to the man I spoke to at Hess Brothers, couldn't have been bought anywhere else; the label made that a certainty. But he remembered no one of Donna's description. The police Missing Persons records carried no description that fit Donna. As far as Allentown went, she had been a blank.

Next stop: the bus company.

Donna had told me she'd come out of her dream at the start of a thirty-minute rest stop, and that the driver had said they were about three hours from Washington. Because buses make both ten-minute and thirty-minute stops, there were only a few places left that might have fit the description. One of them had been the place where Donna Linfoot had begun her amnetic travels.

That part of it was routine: I checked bus companies, I checked drivers. It went on for longer than I liked, and a good deal longer than you want to hear about. But I came up with a night driver on one run who did remember "the girl with the nightmare"—the girl he'd awakened because, when the bus stopped, she seemed to be having a pretty bad dream. "Tossing around and moaning—you know, like that," he said. When he'd awakened her, she'd taken one look at his uniform and, in his words, "thrown a wingding."

Where had she got on? He had no idea. After all, he told me, that had been a month before, or better; he felt he was doing well to remember the girl at all. And she just hadn't registered before that nightmare; the bus

The bus driver's memory began at the same point Donna's did.

I did find out one thing, though: I found out where she'd gotten her name.

The name of the bus driver was Don Linfoot.

I went back to Donna with that much information, and perhaps it was the tiny bit she needed to begin recalling some of her past.

She was still amnesic; she didn't remember who she was, or what the dream meant, or anything else of that sort. But, very subtly, she had begun to relax. I had a hunch that simply talking to her, making it nice and easy, would toss up a little information I could use.

So we talked. I spun some quiet "when I was a kid" yarns and, hardly noticing what she was doing, Donna began on the same sort of thing.

"I used to—I think, anyhow, I used to run away from home occasionally," she said, part way through that long talk.

I kept it casual. "Get far?"

"No," she said. "But I had a handicap. My mother wouldn't let me cross streets, so all I could do was go around in circles."

It seemed to be all I was doing, too. I'd turned up a little, but nothing that did me much good. I kept the conversation going, hoping for any break. Gradually, a picture began to emerge: a large northern city in which she had grown up (she remembered heavy traffic, street cars, snow, ice in the winter). I kept the talk concentrated on the city for a bit. Somewhere, there was a key....

"There was a park," she said. "My mother used to take me to play there, sometimes."

"Big place?"

"Well—fairly big. It seemed big then, anyhow."

Very, very casually, I said: "What was the name of the park?"

She shook her head. "I don't remember." But her voice was still relaxed, still light. "Maybe it didn't even have a name. It was only three squares away, but I couldn't go unless my mother or somebody helped me across the streets. And that's all I remember."

I had my jackpot then, of course. I knew where Donna Linfoot had come from.

Philadelphia.

My mind is stuffed with odd information, at least partly on the basis that you never know when some bit is going to come in handy. One oddity came in handy then:

Philadelphia is the only city in which blocks are called squares.

Pinning down the name of the city let a bit more light in, but it was all in the area of Donna's childhood. Beyond that, she simply could not go; whatever barrier had been set up, whatever the dream had originally meant, was still working.

And she was still living in terror. A gun . . . someone being killed. . . .

And Philadelphia. It struck me that the Linfoot case was certainly a traveling job.

The police Missing Persons Bureau probably had

her name, and a few current details. The problem was to get it without telling them I knew the girl's whereabouts. True, I wasn't legally obligated to give that information to the police unless it could be established that she had committed a crime and that I had knowledge of it; but I didn't want to bring a lawyer along, somehow: the notion didn't seem to make for free and easy conversation.

At last, I realized I had a simple entry. I told the officer at Missing Persons that I was from Tracers Company (true) and that I was interested in any records dealing with a girl of Donna Linfoot's description (also true). If the officer wanted to deduce from that the idea that I was searching for Donna Linfoot, that was his business; I certainly hadn't told him anything of the sort.

And Missing Persons turned her up for me. They'd had her on file for nearly six months: she was wanted in a homicide case.

When I heard that, what was left of my hair nearly turned dead white. I hope I didn't show just how worried I was, but the only thing I could do was to continue talking and hope for some more information.

And if it turned out that she was guilty of murder. . . .

Frankly, I didn't know then what I was going to do; and I don't know now.

Briefly: her name was Elizabeth Mirring. She'd lived with her father all of her life, and she'd managed to meet a young man and fall in love with him. The young man was "unacceptable" to Elizabeth's father, and there were months of gradually intensifying strain, argument, fighting. . . .

As far as the police could reconstruct matters, the young man had been invited to the Mirring house by the father. An argument, of course, had started between them, and the argument had reached brand new heights.

The young man had shot and killed Elizabeth's father.

Elizabeth herself had broken down and been taken to a hospital; the search for her was simply the search for a witness. She'd walked out of the hospital and disappeared.

The trial had been held without her. The young man had been found guilty of second-degree murder.

But the search for Elizabeth Mirring was still in effect.

I took that much information—feeling more relieved than I'd imagined I could feel, now that the dream had been explained without making the girl a murderess—and telegraphed it to "Donna Linfoot's" Washington address. It occurred to me while I was doing that that the police reconstruction of the crime didn't have to be accurate. It was still possible that Elizabeth had committed the murder, and that her fiance had been snarled up in the subsequent investigation and been convicted on good, but not 100-percent-solid, evidence. (There is almost never such a thing as 100-percent-solid evidence.) The reply to my telegram would establish one possibility or the other: if "Donna" called off the hunt, she was very probably guilty of murder. If she didn't . . . then she wasn't. All according to our original agreement.

And there I'd be—trying to decide what to do. . . .

As it happens, I never had to decide.

I waited twelve hours for an answer to my wire. Then I set up a very fast check for the "Linfoot" apartment in Washington.

"Donna"—Elizabeth Mirring—was gone.

Maybe the shock of finding out what had happened had started her off again.

Maybe she'd committed the murder, remembered it when she read the telegram, and felt she had to run.

Maybe. . . .

Well, as I said, it may be the oddest case we've ever handled.

There's only one thing I wish I were sure of.

Do I, or don't I, want to know why, after receiving my telegram, she disappeared?

7
NO PATTERN

There are some cases, of course, that don't quite fit into a neat storytelling pattern; it's sort of a shame that Tracers Company is a real-life private investigative firm instead of a TV show, or a shelf of novels. Some of the cases in our files are labelled "unfinished business," and others are just plain odd. There are times when we finish a case and discover an ending we didn't want to know about.
    Cases like these. . . .

    Well, here's a man who stands to inherit thirty thousand dollars under the terms of an uncle's will.

Clearly, that's a man we want to find. And, just as clearly, that's a man who ought to be glad to be found. Certainly nobody was going to make matters any more troublesome for us than they had to be. . . .

Except that this man didn't bother to think twice—or, for all I know, even once. The result is that he's still unfound—entirely because we were ready and willing to give him just what he wanted.

He took quite a bit of looking for in the first place, but we managed finally to trace him to a flophouse in Chicago. He didn't have either money or a steady job, and we gave the address of the place, and the fact that the man was using his real name, to the attorney for the estate, the man who'd hired us.

The attorney phoned the flophouse and left a message at the desk for the man we'd located.

And the man promptly disappeared again.

That time, he did a good, solid job of it, and hasn't turned up, or been heard from since.

As closely as we could figure matters out when we put everything together, the story went like this:

The flophouse inhabitant did retain an interest in his old family home—there had once been money in the family (and in a few cases there still was, as witness the uncle whose death had started our hunt). That old home represented to him the only truly pleasant part of his life, though he no longer stayed there.

Some years before we entered the picture, he was pressured to sell off his interest in the place. He refused. Violently. He apparently went on refusing until the pressure got too much for him, whereupon he left the home behind it, retaining his interest and so holding on to his dream, and decided to disappear.

He must have figured that the attorney who'd left him a message was just one more guy trying to get him to sign away his rights in the estate. He didn't want to do that, and he didn't want to be bothered anymore. So....

So he disappeared for good—so far, anyhow. (Anybody—anybody at all—can be found, sooner or later. Our file stays open. But this case isn't one I'd care to put a time limit on.)

If he'd stayed around long enough to talk to the attorney, he'd have taken his inheritance, and with it he could have bought out all other holders of interest in the family home—kept it, refurbished it, and lived there for the rest of his life.

But he just didn't bother to think.

One case I remember was solved after one solid year of searching—solved within forty yards of the home from which a fifteen-year-old girl had run away.

She'd just taken off one night, and, since the house was right up against a patch of woods nearly big enough to qualify as a forest, the girl's parents called in not only the local police but the Scouts, professional trackers, amateur helpers who ended up being numbered in the hundreds . . . and Tracers Company.

The girl, we finally found, hadn't wanted to run away. She'd wanted to kill herself, and she'd succeeded: she'd gone into those woods, climbed a tree, arranged a rope and hanged herself.

Searchers had gone past her body from the first day. But nobody had bothered to look *up*.

And here's one we didn't handle. Didn't have to; but I still like to think about it, once in a while. Maybe it compensates, a little, for cases like that suicide—cases where you don't really want the answer you get. Frankly, I'm very fond of the answer I got in the Starr case. . . .

We got a call from Mr. Starr (let's call him; it isn't his name), a well-known show business personality. Mr. Starr's life was a little complicated, though nothing special for show business, I suppose; he'd been married and divorced, and his son by his first marriage had been living with the ex-Mrs. Starr, who had custody of her boy.

Over the summer, though, the son had come to stay with Mr. Starr. And Mr. Starr took the boy on a one-week trip to Europe (where Mr. Starr had a few contracts to fulfill). While in England, the son met some people his own age and decided, once and for all and all at once, that he wanted to be with them.

He wanted (in short) to make the British scene. Unfortunately, he was enrolled as a freshman in a good Eastern college, starting that fall. (Would you believe it was my alma mater? No charge for the coincidence.)

Well, as far as he was concerned this new desire didn't seem to make any problems: all there was to do was to forget about the college and start life over again with his new British friends. But—back in the States, when Mr. Starr and his son returned—the Starrs just couldn't be made to see things that way.

He argued with them, even worked out a complex plan to go to school in England, and got nowhere rapidly . . . and then, on the Sunday before Labor Day, he vanished.

Mr. Starr was worried. He knew the boy had been unhappy, and thought he'd be making a try to get back to England.

Mrs. Starr, though—or, rather, the ex-Mrs. Starr—was frantic. The boy, she said, was capable of anything. Anything at all.

(She'd been sending him to a psychiatrist for two years. I assume that he needed the psychiatric care, but to get from that assumption to the sort of statement his frenzied mother was making is a longer step than, perhaps, most people realize.)

"Anything," she insisted, included suicide. The boy, deeply unhappy (she was sure), had killed himself. We had to find the body—or, in case we were exceptionally speedy and lucky, and reached the boy before he'd breathed his last, we were to keep him alive, to notify the parents. . . .

After a little bit of this when I got together with Mr. and Mrs. Starr, Mr. Starr started getting frantic too. He knew about the psychiatrist (he'd been paying the bills), and he was just worried enough to begin to think, when his ex-wife put the notion in his head, that the step from a psychiatric patient to an immediate potential suicide is a very, very short one. It generally isn't—

but the Starrs were hard to convince.

As I began to get the whole picture, it seemed clear to me that the boy was going to come back before too long, and that any work we did on the case would be wasted motion. The difficulty was in convincing the parents of these facts.

Finally, I remember, I asked Mr. Starr what sort of razor his son used.

He gave me the answer I'd hoped for: "Electric."

I told him to check the medicine cabinet.

"The razor's gone," he told me.

"So he took the razor," I said. "That means either that he's planning to live, or else he's planning to kill himself with that razor; in any other decision, he'd have left it at home. And let me tell you: he'll have a hell of a tough job cutting his throat with an electric razor."

That, Mr. Starr understood. I told him to calm down, and gave him an idea of what I thought would happen.

Then I asked him to have his ex-wife call me—and she did, two days later.

By then, she'd calmed down, too: it seems that the son had "disappeared" by driving out to take a good long look at that Eastern college.

According to his mother, he said: "You know, it doesn't look too bad. I guess I'll give it a try for a year."

As far as I know, he's still in college. I don't know whether he's still going to a psychiatrist, but if he'd been thinking along the lines his parents had outlined to me, I'd be the very first to hope he was still having couch sessions.

83   No Pattern

Anybody who thinks he can cut his throat with an electric razor—well, a guy like that is *really* crazy.

8
DON'T TAKE ANY WOODEN INDIANS

Tracers Company, at one time or another, has been asked to find almost anything.

Once, though, and just once, we got a request that surprised even our nonsurprisable office. We were asked to find a wooden Indian—a *particular* wooden Indian.

We succeeded, too—even though we failed.

Barney Lewis came to us a little hesitantly. He was a nice-looking guy in his early thirties, and he looked a little uncertain about visiting the office of a private investigator—a little more uncertain, even, than the usual client who has the TV and movie ideas about private investigators tacked firmly inside his head. It took him a minute or more to begin with: "It's about my wife."

I asked him: "Is she missing?" and he thought about that for a bit, and didn't quite shake his head.

"Well, I suppose you might say so," he told me at last. "She's—well, she's lost her memory."

It took him quite a time to get the whole story out. Mrs. Lewis was in a sanitarium. A month before, she'd had a baby, the baby had been born dead, and the shock had sent her right into a sort of catalepsy. Barney Lewis got that far, and blinked, and then went on very slowly:

"She just kind of . . . froze up. She—doesn't even know me. But—"

A long time passed. I said: "But what?"

"Well . . . the doctor there thinks that, if she could be reminded of the good times, the times before . . . before all this happened . . . then she might remember again. Come out of it, I mean."

Even then, it didn't sound like one of our usual jobs; in fact, I couldn't quite see where we were going to fit in. Rapidly, then, it started to sound even weirder.

"I thought of something," Barney said, "but when I got back to the old neighborhood, everything had changed. Nobody knows what happened to the Indian." To make it absolutely clear, he added: "The Indian's gone."

The old neighborhood, he told me, was in New York, up around 177 Street. And the Indian?

"The night we met, it was raining," Barney said. "We were both standing under an awning, and this Indian was standing there. He had only one ear. So we kind of—talked about—about that. It ended up with me taking her home, and after that we started having dates, and—"

"I get the picture," I said. "Anyhow, I think I do. Did you ever see this one-eared Indian again?"

Barney nodded. "Sure," he said. "We'd go back there every so often. You know how it is. One night I even carved my initials in him."

That one almost sent me through the ceiling. Barney Lewis had forgotten to mention that he was not talking about a live Indian.

"No, a cigar-store Indian. You know. Didn't I tell you?"

With great restraint, I said: "No."

It developed—speedily, from that point on—that Barney Lewis wanted us to find the cigar-store Indian, thinking that the reminder, once brought to her in the sanitarium, would bring his wife back to normal life. As far as I could follow the psychiatric jargon, his idea—or the doctor's idea—sounded O.K. but mostly we get hired to find missing *people*.

There was only one really bright spot I could see about trying to find a missing cigar-store Indian instead.

He couldn't run.

The Indian's description wasn't much to go on. The left ear had been knocked off, and the initials A. R.

and B. L. had been carved in the chest. (Barney Lewis' wife's maiden name had been Anne Rainey.) The Indian had been standing, when last seen, in front of a cigar store—then part of a chain of stores, and, when we started looking, out of business.

The store's stock had been absorbed by another store in the chain; that much was easy to dig up. When we got to the head office of the chain, though, someone remembered that Indian. It had been sold separately— for five dollars—to an artist. A woman named Karolyn Shafter.

Finding Miss Shafter was simple; she was in the phone book. She was a sculptor, the Moddest of the Mod, and she was entirely uninterested in wooden Indians. After quite a lot of talking back and forth, most of which was simply confusing (unless, I suppose, you happen to be a Mod sculptor), she did remember buying him. It had seemed like rather a novel idea at the time, but having the Indian around all the time had become boring; she'd sold him.

Anyhow, she went on, she thought she had. She'd got rid of the Indian one way or another, that much was for sure. And she couldn't be bothered to remember how.

A lot of my job is simple patience, and an assignment like that one used up my stock for the week. Finally, after a lot more conversation, she did remember.

"I paid a junk man two dollars to haul it away," she told me.

The junk man, it developed, was named Sam. And

there her information stopped, once and for all.

Three junkyards later, I met Sam Barra, a little, balding man with tiny eyes and a hoarse voice. He remembered the Indian, all right. "I had one—sure. Some time or another. It don't make it worth my while to look for it; who buys things like that these days?"

I asked him about the initials and the missing ear.

He shrugged. "Could be," he said, "and could be not. Who notices?"

So I asked him to try to find it. He looked at me as if I'd gone crazy.

I told him the whole story, but Sam Barra wasn't interested.

"It sounds like nothing," he said, "a nothing business. What's in it for me, to get mixed up with a thing like that? A real nothing business, that's all."

I went over everything again, and I managed to persuade him that finding the Indian, in the mounds of junk covering his yard, would be important. "Lewis hasn't get much money, though," I said. "You see, it's his wife—"

"His wife?" Barra said. "What's it matter to me, his wife? It's not *my* wife, is it?" He shrugged at me. "So, then. He wants it"— he waved his hands—"he pays for it. Believe me. I'm in this business for my health?"

At any rate, Sam Barra was, he told me, willing to look. I left that ramshackle office of his, stuck away in a corner of the junkyard—but I left very slowly.

After the door had closed, I could still hear him moving around. He picked up the phone. I heard him dial.

"I want the number for Stage Props, Inc."

And when I heard that much, I went right on leaving—about five times as fast.

Stage Props, unfortunately, tracked down the Indian.

It had been in a warehouse fire, a year and more before.

The special Indian Barney Lewis' wife needed had gone up in a record pile of smoke.

And that, it seemed, was that.

Strangely enough, the next idea wasn't mine; it was Sam Barra's. He called Barney Lewis and told him he had the Indian, and was willing to sell it—for only seventy-five dollars. Barney checked with us, and I told him the truth of what we'd found; but Sam's idea kept it from being a total loss.

It was obvious that Sam was simply going to carve the initials on the chest of any prop Indian he could find, knock off one ear, and sell the result as the original.

But the difference might not matter. In Ann Lewis' condition, she might not even be able to tell the difference; the substitute Indian might be just as good.

Barney Lewis didn't have seventy-five spare dollars —but of course he didn't need anything like that sum. Stage Props, Inc. sold us an Indian for the same price they'd just charged Sam Barra: seven dollars.

The carpentry work took less than an hour. Weathering a very shiny, new-looking prop Indian to the beat-up condition of the original took a little longer.

But it worked. My accountant tells me we lost money on that job, but, you know—the job was worth it. The sound of Ann Lewis' voice when she called to thank us—and the sound of Barney's voice as well—was a kind of payment my accountant couldn't enter in a ledger.

But—as Sam Barra might never understand—it was payment, and good payment, all the same.

INTERLUDE II

It happens at least three times a week: somebody calls me and offers to pay me for instructions on how to disappear successfully.

When an abandoned wife says: "I know him. He wouldn't run away of his own free will," she's wrong. She doesn't know him—because he has.

When a person starts telling me that They are intercepting his mail, I tell him I'll take care of everything—and I walk him very soothingly to the door.

Once, I appeared on a radio show with the author of a series of police detective novels, and with one of the foremost authorities on Sherlock Holmes. The moderator described a problem. The author told how his police detectives would solve it; the authority told how Holmes would have gone about the matter.

Then I described how it would really be done.

The stock-in-trade of a con man is charm. Without it, he'd be out of business faster than any enforcement officer could get to him.

People who use amnesia as their excuse for having left home nearly always think the idea is original with them. It seems to be original with an awful lot of people.

It figures: the theme song of the radio show "Mr. Keene, Tracer of Lost Persons," was: "Some Day I'll Find You."

If I wanted to disappear, I'd probably go to Pittsburgh.

Interlude II

I could never understand why anybody would hire a private detective for any amount per day. The faster he solved the case, the less money he'd make.

One of my favorite relaxations is watching a private eye movie or TV show. It's so entirely unlike my daily work.

9
HOW COULD SHE DO THIS TO US?

There have been runaway teen-agers since long before Tracers Company was founded—since, in fact, a long time before anybody had ever invented the word "teen-ager." But—a fact which is guaranteed to surprise very few people, I'm afraid—the pattern, these days, is changing, changing radically and with great speed.

Up until about 1960, the typical teen-age runaway looked like this: he was a boy, about sixteen years old, and worried about low marks or something of the sort. He'd just tossed some clothes into a suitcase, scraped up a few dollars and taken himself off for happier places in a thoughtless hurry.

Within a week or so, he'd be on the phone to his folks, asking for bus fare right on back home, having discovered in the interim that the life of a footloose wanderer isn't exactly the Earthly Paradise.

Now, though, everything has changed: age, sex, reasons, all at once. The typical runaway now is a year or so younger—say, an average age of fifteen. That runaway is, for the first time, likelier to be a girl than a boy.

And the reasons...

Well, a good many of them seem to have the same attitude, the same rationale: they're tired of being parasites and not contributing anything real to society, and they're off to help bring about a new and better world.

Nobody can fault the ambition expressed, but the process of realizing it usually isn't thought out any too well. Their aspirations may be high, but these kids are still fifteen years old—with all the lack of experience and the too-rapid, oversimplified process of judgment that age implies.

Only one thing hasn't changed: the parents are still left asking the same question: "We gave her everything she wanted—how could she do this to us?"

It seems to me that the answer is where answers are sometimes found: right in the question itself. "... to *us.*" It might clarify matters a little if those parents were to ask, instead, "... how could she do this to *herself?*"

But, then, if they'd done that, the odds were that there wouldn't have been a runaway in the first place.

Take Susan Johnson, for instance.

She'd been gone for over four weeks. The day after she left, her parents got a letter from her, postmarked from Manhattan. (The Johnsons lived in a fairly nearby suburb.) The letter told them that she wanted no more of their "materialistic indulgences"; she wanted to go out into the world and help mankind (kind of help or specimens of mankind not specified), her parents shouldn't worry about her; and she'd be home again in three years—right after her eighteenth birthday.

The Johnsons had given the letter to the police, and they'd been hard at work. But, with time piling up and no results coming in, the parents came to Tracers Company, and I went out to their home with the stirrings of an idea.

The neighborhood was fashionable, tree lined, everything any addict of advertisements could dream of. "Materialistic indulgences" was one way to describe it—if you were a fifteen-year-old girl who'd never gotten more than the simplest shiny surface of that world to deal with. The surface just wasn't enough. It never was; it never will be.

It wasn't enough for my job, either. The police had started with the note and the Johnsons' story and description. I wanted to go one step further.

Nobody had taken a good look at Susan's room.

That was my idea. I, too, had to get under the surface, and Susan's room might give me the clues to get there.

The first thing that caught, and held my attention

was the desk and the bookshelf above it. The shelf was arranged in what appeared to be no particular order, but the accidents of simply stacking one book up, and then a new book next to it, gave me what looked like a chronological sketch of Susan's world, of Susan's thinking. The shelf started with *Little Women* at one end and culminated with *The Negro Experience* at the other. I've seldom seen any physical clue as open, as obvious and as compact.

But it was a clue to Susan, and only minimally to where she might have gone, and what she might be doing. It stirred a few ideas, of course, but they were reasonably non specific. I'd gotten about all I was going to get out of the bookshelf.

So I went over to the desk. A schoolbag lay on it—apparently undisturbed in all the four weeks since she'd been gone.

When there's no simpler opening (and, a lot of the time, there isn't), you start to track a runaway by looking around at the back trail—the last point or so the subject visited before taking off. Almost always, the subject will have dropped something, left something behind, taken something along (as in the case of Mr. Starr and his son's electric razor) to give you a clue.

That point is pretty much elementary. I've even seen it stated in mystery novels. But nobody had looked at Susan's back trail, even when there was nowhere else to go.

All right. The schoolbag wasn't going to be undisturbed any longer. I opened it, and fished out the various notebooks inside it and the loose-leaf folder

Susan used for her lecture notes. The folder was divided into sections according to subject; the notes seemed to be well organized; the penmanship was neat and clear.

All of which was surface and gave me, at first glance, nothing more.

But I was determined that the book was going to tell me something. The arrangement of books on a shelf had told me a lot about Susan. Her own notebook was going to tell me more; and I wasn't going to stop with the first glance—with, in other words, the surface.

The second look, as I leafed through the folder, paid off. I noticed a name:

Alfred.

It was written in the margin, and seemed to have no connection with anything else at all. I went on through the folder, checking more carefully this time.

Alfred again.
Alfredo.
Alfredo Mendoza.
Alfred Mendoza.
Susan J. Mendoza.
Senora Susan Mendoza.

The surface had cracked. In a sense, there hadn't been anyone left to question (after I'd heard the parents' story, seen the letter) except Susan herself. So, I'd done that. And she was beginning to give me some answers. Now, with the answers for ammunition, I could begin again questioning her parents.

"Did Susan have a boyfriend named Alfred?"

Mrs. Johnson was downstairs in the kitchen. Mr. Johnson had gone off to work, leaving instructions that he be called if anything developed that needed his immediate attention. Mrs. Johnson thought about the question for a minute and looked up at me.

"No. Not that I know of."

But the one thing that was clear, as in such cases it nearly always is clear, was that the parents had probably never known of much of Susan's life, or asked about it. I went through a few more questions, looking for an opening.

"She mostly dated boys from the school here," Mrs. Johnson told me. "And almost always she went on double dates with her cousin, Betty."

"Betty?" It looked like my opening.

The girl lived two blocks away. At my request, Mrs. Johnson had her on the telephone within minutes, and in not much longer than that Betty rang the Johnsons' front door bell. She looked quite a lot like Susan, if I could go by the Johnsons' snapshots of their daughter, and she was two months older, no more.

And, of course, I was an adult. I was the enemy. I was the guy over thirty, the guy you never trust.

So: I told Betty that I knew she wanted to do everything she could to relieve the agony her aunt and uncle, Mr. and Mrs. Johnson, were going through over Susan's disappearance. I made it very clear, and very sympathetically plain, that we were all also concerned with the simple fact of Susan's well-being; if anything happened to her, the happening was going to remain with everyone concerned—including Betty—for the rest of their lives.

It was, more or less, the sort of thing Betty must have expected to hear; but it shook her more than she expected it to. *The rest of their lives* can sound like a very long time, even when you're fifteen.

I gave her a while to think about that. And I gave her a while to anticipate the sort of thing I was going to say next. "If you have any idea where she might have gone, or if you think you might know anything that could be at all helpful. . . ." Sure. She was totally prepared for that.

So I didn't say it.

Instead, I asked her: "Who's Alfredo Mendoza?"

She blinked and stared at me, defenses down, gone and forgotten. Then, with no more than an occasional question by me tossed in to keep the flow going, she began to talk.

Each Saturday morning for three months, she and Susan had been allowed to go in to Manhattan to attend art classes at the Museum of Modern Art. (Mrs. Johnson nodded agreement; I saw that out of the corner of my eye. Betty wasn't looking at Susan's mother, and I didn't want to remind her that Mrs. Johnson was even in the room. I didn't even shift my eyes.)

Of course they met some boys in the class. (Mrs. Johnson began to pay a more strained variety of attention. I didn't look at her.) Alfredo was one of those boys.

The last four times they'd been to the city, Susan and Alfredo had gone down to Greenwich Village; Alfredo knew some "real artists" there and introduced

Susan to them. (For all I know, incidentally, they may have been real artists, without the quotation marks—to the great surprise of many people, quite a lot of good work gets done down in the Village.)

These people lived in a "commune sort of thing," ten of them: six male, four female. They shared everything. "It's the only way true artists can live," Betty told me. (It may not be necessary to mention that, by that time, Mrs. Johnson was sitting bolt upright. I kept my gaze concentrated on Betty.) Susan always met Betty back at the museum by deadline time, and they caught the same bus back home. But on the last trip Susan had said she'd made up her mind. She wanted to live with Alfredo and the others.

Betty was scared to tell anyone about it, she said; besides, of course, it wasn't anything you could tell older people. They wouldn't understand.

Somewhere along the line, just through listening, I'd managed to show Betty that I might, just might (even if I were a doddering ancient), understand.

I got in touch with our "hippie" contact in the East Village, a young man who'd worked with us several times before—and whose language I could talk, a fact which Betty, even after her long story, might never have believed. This time, I told him, I was giving him an easy one.

"A runaway?"

"Sure," I told him, and began to give him the picture.

And the next morning, after he'd phoned me, I called Mr. and Mrs. Johnson and told them where Susan was living. From that point on, the job belonged to them, and to Susan; I'd been hired, not to run anybody's life, but to provide information.

And—sure, I can talk to the kids; I have contacts in the East Village and elsewhere.

All the same, when I put down the phone I was calling from home—I went into the den where Laura, my twelve-year-old, was performing her latest guitar piece for her mother and her father, her sister and her brother.

And I wondered. . . .

10
AS SIMPLE AS THAT

Most of the cases I deal with have some sort of lesson tacked on to them—a fact which you may have noticed already. I don't put it there; at most, I just notice that it has been tacked on. Sometimes it's a straight professional lesson; sometimes it's a little wider in application.

The case Rupert Prince brought me certainly had a lesson attached to it; but, as far as I can figure out, the lesson never was learned. Of course, I'll never be entirely sure—since it certainly wasn't me doing the learning. All I had to worry about was a tough and complicated job. It was Rupert Prince who had the learning to do.

In fact, he'd been studying, if that's the word I

want, for a long, long time. The subject was marriage, and my client was more of less an expert: after all, he'd been married four times, and was about to make it five. The trouble was that the courses were beginning to cost more than he could afford: the alimony payments for wives number one, two and three could be managed, but wife number four was not about to let Mr. Prince go tuition free, and that last little burden was making everything seem terribly expensive all of a sudden.

Happily, he told himself after giving the matter a great deal of thought, there was a way out. Wife number four had been divorced before she'd married him. Suppose, though, that her divorce hadn't been quite final. In that case, of course, her marriage to him hadn't even been legal in the first place, and the whole question of alimoney could be allowed to slide quietly and completely out of sight.

Now when Rupert Prince—once more, as is true throughout this book, the client's real name is in my files, where it belongs, and not on the printed page—when Prince came to us, he'd managed to refine his brainstorm down to the point at which someone could go to work on it. In fact, he wrapped it up for me in just one single sentence:

"All I want you to do is to turn up evidence that my ex-wife's ex-husband, Charles Ringgold (also an invented name, of course), wasn't a bona fide resident of Nevada for the six-week residency period when he got his divorce—it's as simple as that."

Why is it that the really tough ones can always be

put in such small nutshells? It sounded, to Rupert Prince, like the easiest job in the world.

It didn't sound like that to me. To be perfectly frank, I got a bit confused by "ex-wife's ex-husband," and by the time I had that much straightened out I began to see the size of the job we were taking on.

The subject, Charles Ringgold, was a name to us, and very little more. Prince didn't know a great deal about him, and wasn't even sure what, if anything, he did for a living. It was a dead-certain bet that we were not going to get any cooperation from the ex-Mrs. Prince who had once been the ex-Mrs. Ringgold.

We started in Nevada, where the Ringgolds had been divorced—we had to; there wasn't anyplace else to start. And a check of the records there did show up our Mr. Ringgold, filing for divorce on a particular date and stating (that's the way they like it said out there) that he had every intention of remaining within the state indefinitely. If his intentions held out for six weeks, fine. After that he could file the intentions under Miscellaneous, collect his divorce, and clear out.

Of course, it was perfectly possible that he hadn't stayed on for the full six-week period: sitting around with nothing much to do is wearing on the nerves. The difficulty was: if he *had* skipped out a bit early, how were we supposed to find out about it—and, what's more, prove it? For a while there, I wondered if anyone, ever, had checked every hotel, motel, cabin and boarding-house register in all fifty states—because that looked like the only chance of our establishing anything at all.

You see, neither Nevada nor any other state requires a passport to enter (so long as you enter it from somewhere else in the United States). This is a great convenience, among other things, most of the time; what it looked like at that moment was a simple curse.

Checking every hotel, motel, and so forth in Nevada alone would be a longer job than any I care to think about—and if Ringgold turned out to be unregistered anywhere for part or all of that six-week period what had we proved? For all we knew, the guy liked to sleep in his car, someplace off the highway. Or he'd managed to register under a false name, which many people do for various reasons, and which isn't a criminal act unless it's "for purposes of deception"—which brought us right back to where we started. It would be a little difficult to show the purposes of an action of Ringgold's, if we couldn't turn up Ringgold.

He'd arrived in Nevada; we had that much. Now, how were we going to get something more? And what imaginable "something more" would do us any good? We weren't after a suspicion, or even a fact. We were after legal proof—which is a bit harder to locate than a nice simple fact, if only because it has to stand up before a few lawyers without shaking itself to pieces.

So we began to run a few checks on Charles Ringgold. There are reference works like *Who's Who*, and there are listings and reference books covering various professions as well. I was crossing my fingers (between flipping pages and making phone calls) that Ringgold would turn out to be a professional man of some sort, because in that case, and perhaps only in that case, we had a faint lead to work with.

And we pulled up lucky—after picking reference books, cross-checking lists and everything else apart for what seemed like thirty years (it was more like thirty days): Charles Ringgold—the Charles Ringgold we were after, who'd been married to our Mr. Prince's wife number four, and who'd been divorced on a given date—turned out to be an engineer.

Understand: we still didn't know whether or not he had left Nevada any earlier than the law required. But we had the beginning of an idea about where to look in order to find out.

An engineer, like many professionals, requires a license. And many professional licensing requirements differ from state to state. So....

If Ringgold had left Nevada early . . .

and *if* he'd become impatient and decided to take up work in another state . . .

and *if* he hadn't been previously licensed in that state . . .

well, then, just maybe we'd found our client's out.

And, as it turned out, we had.

A license application for Charles Ringgold turned up in Arizona—dated a full three days before that six-week stay was up!

It was beautiful, just beautiful. As evidence, it couldn't have been much better. The application had his signature, and (in his own handwriting) his residence address in Arizona, and the date.

All we had to do was to get the application copied, and then get it certified by the issuing agency—and that was just as much of a cinch as it sounds.

Then we went back to Mr. Prince with it.

Mr. Prince was, of course, grateful. But he couldn't quite understand why he had to pay so much for such a simple job. After all, we'd only had to turn up one little piece of paper, wasn't that so?

I tried to explain to him just how many pieces of paper we'd picked that necessary little one out of—tried to give him some idea of the size of the haystack we'd gone through to find his needle.

But he still didn't see what was so tough about finding a simple piece of evidence. "At least," he said, a bit grudgingly, "you did the job. I will say that. Why, the two companies I hired before I came to you couldn't even do a simple little thing like this."

Simple?

Well, there are times when I know just how Sherlock Holmes felt after explaining some lovely interlocking set of deductions to Watson or Lestrade, when he heard them say: "Why, of course! It's obvious!"

That lesson I was speaking of. . . .

On the latest evidence, I think it's still unlearned. Mr. Prince's name hit the papers recently—complete with a picture of him aboard his yacht. He was (the story said) making plans for his forthcoming marriage—in Reno, I think it was going to be. Unless I've missed one or two in the intervening years, that makes wife number six.

It also means that he's a bit richer than he was when he came to us—or, at any rate, that he's figured out a way to manage four alimony payments, at last. I hope he has; I'm not sure I want to depend on being that lucky ever again, if he gets another bright idea and comes on back.

11
HAPPY ANNIVERSARY

The last time I counted, Tracers Company was receiving about three hundred requests to find "missing" husbands for every one request to locate a "missing" wife. This, of course, is a reflection of the fact that more husbands disappear than wives. Some people, upon hearing that statistic, kind of laugh and say things like: "If it happened to me, I'd say Hallelujah and forget about the whole thing."

Of the wives who do run away, the typical one is something like this: married by age eighteen; first child born within one year; two more children in next five years; by thirty-five, she is convinced that the world has passed her by and, unless she does something about it *now*, she will miss out on everything. So, she takes off.

She first goes through a whole physical transformation (she thinks) including a new hairdo (and color), a new style of dressing and, for the first time in her adult life, a new style of living. Very quickly, however, some realities start to set in. She has to get a job . . . and all she's qualified to do is work as a waitress or as a check-out girl in a super market, jobs she has been training for during the previous seventeen years.

In other words, it's a pretty discouraging experience. And really not romantic at all.

But every once in a while, someone comes up with a new twist on the old theme. Which always makes me realize that there is that exceptional person, and not all categories of people should be simply assigned to just that—categories.

Walter Burgess was a banker in New Orleans. His wife had been missing for twenty years. She'd disappeared on their honeymoon.

This is what Walter Burgess told me: He had graduated from college and gone to work at the bank. It was convenient—his father was president of the bank. He liked the work well enough. But most of all, he liked the time he had to spend in the data processing department. There was a beautiful girl there named Caroline Bard.

At that point, he handed me a picture. He was right—she was a beauty. I told Mr. Burgess that she must have made a lovely bride. He said she certainly did, and he pointed out that she had made her wedding gown herself. (Her mother had been a dressmaker. Caroline must have learned the craft from her.)

I asked whether contact had been made with Caroline's mother. Mr. Burgess told me that both her parents had died many years ago.

When I mentioned that twenty years was a long time, that a person's appearance could change a lot, I noticed that he kind of welled up with tears. He got up from his chair and walked around my office for a few moments . . . time enough to regain his composure.

That's when he told me how she disappeared. They were on their way back from their honeymoon. They had been driving cross-country, with no particular itinerary. When they liked a place, they simply stopped there and spent as much time as they wanted to—as much as they could of the two weeks they had to spend.

Just outside of Fort Worth, Texas, they got into an accident.

It was a head-on collision, and the last thing Mr. Burgess remembers before passing out was the fire.

Caroline was badly burned about the face, he told me, but he never did see how bad the damage really was. She had walked out of the hospital before he saw her unbandaged.

In fact, he never saw her again.

I remarked that, obviously, she had left of her own free will. Why didn't he just leave it that way?

He gave me the most acceptable answer there is: "She's my wife . . . and I love her."

Mr. Burgess had given me the address at which Caroline Bard had lived before he married her. It was a rooming house for women on Minetta Street in New Orleans. She had never mentioned any relatives.

For twenty years, Walter Burgess had been searching for his wife, and had failed to turn up a single lead to her whereabouts after the hospital in Fort Worth. I had to start from scratch with only two basic facts: her face was badly burned and probably still bore the scars, and she was an expert seamstress.

I decided that my starting point had to be New Orleans. That was where she had been born and raised. Besides, I had nothing else to work on.

One other thought: she *had* been in love with her husband; wouldn't it be reasonable to assume that she might want to be close enough to him to follow his career, even though she couldn't share it?

I contacted one of our agents in New Orleans and instructed him to get started on the standard procedures of researching local public and private records . . . and to meet me at the New Orleans airport the following day.

The next afternoon, we started making the rounds of dress shops and department stores. We showed Caroline's picture and gave her physical description, but we came up with no leads or clues at all.

After two and a half days of that sort of thing, we were absolutely no further along in the search than when we had started. Of course, we'd considered the possibility that Caroline had used her maiden name or her married name. The Bureau of Vital Statistics told us that no Caroline Bard or Burgess had died in the twenty-year period that had passed. It occurred to me: maybe she'd changed her name to something else. I knew her date of birth (her husband had given me that), and I knew she'd been born in New Orleans.

I also knew that people sometimes used their mother's maiden name—when it became necessary or desirable to use one other than their own.

Under the date, April 23, 1926, there was no listing for the birth of Caroline Bard.

However, there was a record of the birth on that date of Cara Bardonelli: father, Giuseppe; mother, Anna Trissino.

It had to be.

Back to the routine research again. But this time, a death record for Anna Bardonelli was uncovered. It showed that she had died only three years earlier. (Didn't Mr. Burgess say that Caroline's parents had been dead for many years?) The death certificate showed the address at which Anna Bardonelli had lived until the end.

I went to the address, a rather old apartment building. I rang the superintendent's bell. He could speak very little English (and I can speak just about no French). I showed him Caroline's picture. He shook his head—no.

I knocked on the door of every other apartment in the building. And finally, the confirmation came. The dead woman did have a daughter. Her face was scarred. She'd moved out after her mother died. No one knew where. One woman said she thought that Cara used to work in a dress factory.

Back to the classified telephone directory—under the listing for dresses, wholesale and manufacturers. And I started making the rounds again, too.

I found out that talking to a foreman at a manufacturing plant is a lot different from making an inquiry of the boss lady of a small dressmaking shop.

At the third place I went to—just as I was being unceremoniously ushered out the door by the foreman and a security guard—I caught a glimpse of a woman bent over her sewing machine. She had a badly scarred face. Then the door was slammed in my face.

Ten minutes later, I had the owner of the factory on the phone. After he gave me assurance that I wouln't be tossed out again, I headed back to his plant. His office was on a different floor than the large room in which I'd seen the lady with the scarred face. I explained the whole story to him and he called his personnel department to ask about an employee named Caroline (or Cara, I added) Burgess, Bard or Bardonelli.

Within a few minutes, he got a return call from personnel. No, there was no employee by any of those names. There was a new machine operator, though—she'd been there for only two days—who had the same first name.

She was Cara Trissino.

Of course, Trissino was the maiden name of her mother. The inquiries made over the previous several days must have gotten close to her. She must have left her previous job and taken on this new one . . . under her new name.

I was given her home address.

I called Walter Burgess and told him what I had. He asked whether I would consider meeting him and accompanying him to the address. I bent one of my personal rules, and told him that I would.

When Mr. Burgess showed up, he had a package under his arm. I stood aside as he knocked on the door of his bride's apartment, and handed her a twentieth anniversary present that she didn't even see. Her eyes were too filled with tears.

I must admit that my vision became a little blurred just about then, too.

12
A NICE DULL JOB

Sometimes, of course, Tracers Company runs into a case that looks more or less ordinary. It has none of the private eye trappings at all—no shoot-outs, no vengeful mobsters, or whatever TV is using for suspense this season. It has no wild Texans, no wooden Indians and no electric razors; it hasn't even got much of the sob-story soap opera about it; and, in general, it just isn't a story worth telling, unless you happen to be the person looked for, or the person doing the looking.

But there are exceptions to everything—and the story of Mrs. Greenleaf's will seems to be one of them.

For a change, this one didn't start in my office, but in the office of an attorney—a Mr. Eldridge, I might as well call him. He'd asked me to come over at three to discuss an "estate matter," and to judge from his address and the tone of his voice, I figured he was talking about rather a large estate.

He was. The estimated value was about fourteen million dollars.

When he'd told me that much, I merely nodded. Soberly and quietly. After all, for legal purposes it might just as well have been fourteen dollars, and I certainly shouldn't have looked impressed. I hope I didn't—but I wouldn't bet on it.

Mrs. Greenleaf had recently died, leaving her will in the keeping of Mr. Eldridge. She claimed to be seventy-five years old. The will contained assorted bequests, of assorted types: fifty thousand dollars to her hairdresser, the same to the elevator operator in the apartment-hotel in which she lived (the will characterized this gentleman as "discreet," by the way), the same to Mr. Eldridge's secretary, who'd handled a few personal errands for her and sometimes helped her select clothes, and finally one more fifty-thousand-dollar bequest to a Mr. Epstein, a nice guy who drove a cab and who, once a month, took her up to the cemetery in which her two sisters were buried.

The rest of the money was divided into two trusts. One of them, somewhere in the neighborhood of ten million dollars (a very nice neighborhood, I might add), was set up so that the income from the trust was to be paid to Mrs. Greenleaf's good friend Mr. Kozinsky.

The other one (only three and a half million dollars, if you can bear to think of that as *only*) was to go—in the same manner—to lawyer Eldridge.

(An additional fact or two: both incomes were to continue for the lifetime of the nominees; upon the death of either, his trust was to go to an Institute of Physics—this last stipulation thoughtfully provided by Mrs. Greenleaf in accordance with the dying wish of an alumnus of that school—who, as it happened, had married Mrs. Greenleaf's sister, which is how Mrs. G. got rich in the first place.)

Naturally, Mr. Eldridge was pleased and excited; he almost—in spite of himself—looked it. And when you added it all up, it was awfully hard to blame the man. After all, he'd just turned forty-four, and counted on living to at least seventy. That meant twenty-six years of income . . . at a (conservative) 4 percent . . . makes . . . let's see, now. . . .

About a hundred and forty thousand dollars a year. For twenty-six years.

(If he lived to be over seventy, of course, the same hundred and forty thousand dollars would be paid in every year. It was a nice extra inducement, if he needed one, for a long life-span.)

It didn't seem, at that point, that Mr. Eldridge could be in any trouble. But when he handed me a bulging letter file and began explaining, I began taking notes. The file contained letters, personal address books, and hundreds upon hundreds of little scraps of paper, every one of these last scribbled over or printed with some memorandum or other. Then there were ads clipped from God knows how many years of newspapers and magazines, business cards (a wide and confusing selection), appointment cards for dentists and doctors, invitations to parties and so forth—even a single faded dance program for a long-gone, mist-covered cotillion.

It was a life on paper—the life of a lonely woman who had never, apparently, thrown out anything whatever.

My job?

"I want you to find any next of kin, or any heir-at-law, of Mrs. Greenleaf," Mr. Eldridge told me. "If there is one, and the will is disallowed—which can happen, as you know—then that person is entitled to the entire estate."

All of which might have been, on his part, a fine and selfless gesture.

It might have been. But it's also required by law.

Anyhow: "Oh, by the way," he added as I was about to leave, "if we can establish that she was actually older than she claimed to be, the estate won't have to pay out so much in taxes; it'll be a bigger estate all around." He said something about the length of a life estate dictating the amount of taxes. . . .

Mostly, when someone says "by the way" to me, I tense up. It usually means a problem of quite respectable size is on the way. But that last afterthought didn't look too bad. Maybe, in fact, the job would really be the nice simple one it looked like. Or nearly . . . which is about the most you hope for, in this business.

I was actually at the door when he said "by the

way" again. I tensed again. And that time I was right.

"Her name wasn't really Greenleaf, you know," he said. I didn't bother to tell him I hadn't known. "She added the 'leaf' because it sounded better to her. And—I think you ought to know this—she told me she had no remaining relatives at all."

Wonderful. "Anything else?" I said.

"Well—she was never married," he told me. "She used the 'Mrs.' for—well, for reasons of her own, I suppose."

Marvelous.

A woman named Green, who called herself "Mrs." and had never been married, who quite possibly lied about her age, who claimed to have no relatives. . . .

Sure. A nice simple job.

It wasn't as if I had nothing to start with. I had enough to start with to choke the average private detective; I had that mass of papers. Who was it who said that the difference between a fictional private detective job and a real one is that in the fictional one you have too few clues, in the real one too many? Dashiell Hammett—who may be the only detective-story writer who was once a real-life private detective. And Hammett was about right—anyhow, he seemed to be right about Mrs. Green.

I had a lot of clues—I had that bulging file. I couldn't quite see what good any of it was going to do me, but it provided a fine starting place to look around from, and that night I started looking.

Going through the papers gave me a weird feeling—as if I were entering the secret channels of a life whose owner wouldn't at all have wanted me there. The life went back and back, bringing memories and notes, indecipherable scribbles, block-printed lists of groceries and lists of operas. . . .

It also brought me a preliminary questionnaire issued by the U.S. Government in preparation for the taking of a federal census. Mrs. Greenleaf, who saved everything, had saved that too, and provided me with a real starting point.

I looked it over.

For *place of birth,* she'd written: *New York.*

For *date of birth,* she'd written: *June 24.*

No year.

But I had to figure that the date was right as far as it went; there seemed no reason to change it. And "New York" on a form generally means Manhattan. That headed me for the Vital Statistics records of Manhattan.

Records, though, for what year? Maybe the age she'd claimed was the right one, but her lawyer hadn't seemed to think so. So . . . I did some fast divination, and thought about other cases in which a woman had changed her reported age . . . and fixed on ten years as the most probable jump for her to have made; when she said she was seventy-five, she was really eighty-five. (I wish I could explain how I do this sort of thing—even to me. There are times when I almost believe in telepathy, the Mystic Whosis, or you-name-it, though what any stuff of that sort is doing in the life of a sober, hard-working private investigator I will never know. The easiest explanation is "experience," and it's the one I usually give. It may even be true.)

My divination gave me a probable year: 1878. The trouble with that was the state of the New York Vital Statistics file: though New York has compiled its vital statistics since 1847, the lists up until 1879 (the year after the one I was checking) are kind of haphazard; your chances of finding a given listing is about one in two, or it might be one in three.

Of course, I had (or assumed I had) the advantage of a specific month, day and year.

But. . .

Well, page the Keeper of the Mystic Whosis, I suppose: the record gave me: "–Green, female," and then: "third child born to Frances Johnson and Richard L. Green," born at "Doctor's Hospital," residential address "271 East 23 Street." It all fit. My Mrs. G. had had two sisters, who'd died before her–remember the taxi driver, and the in-case bequest to the Institute of Physics?–which made sense, since, according to the record I now had, they'd been older.

Now, in 1870, eight years before, there'd been a census taken of New York City residents. Blessing the census-takers with all my heart, I dragged out the records.

Why?

Well, the previous two children, according to the 1878 record, were only a year and two years older than my Mrs. G. Maybe–just maybe, so long as the Mystic Whosis was smiling on me anyway–Richard L. Green, their father, had not yet married Frances Johnson in

1870. Maybe he lived at home, in New York City, with his family. Maybe there was a brother or two. . . .

The 1870 census is handwritten. It looks very fancy and impressive and Victorian, once you can see your way through the choking clouds of dust all over it. I saw my way, sneezing and sputtering, to page 371 of Volume 14.

At the top of that page was the name *Richard L. Green.* The census told me that he was seventeen, a student, born in this country.

Most important, it told me that Peter L. Green, Francis L. Green and William L. Green lived in the same household, and that all these latter three were, like Richard, sons of James R. Green and Madeline Stanhope.

So: my Mrs. G. had at least three uncles. Children of such uncles, if any, would be her first cousins. Children of her first cousins would be first cousins once removed—and, whether or not Mrs. G. thought they were relatives, any court was going to. I'd dug up what Mr. Eldridge was going to think of as a disappointing (if necessary) lead—but I was still rather pleased with myself. It wasn't every private investigator who had a Fairy Godmother in such good contact with the Mystic Whosis.

The next few days were spent doing the usual research: papers and papers and papers, files and files and files, material from the census and the Vital Statistics lists and the probate court calendars (for the wills of the uncles involved, etc.). The exciting life of a Private Investigator.

Result: two living first cousins, located in Pennsylvania.

They knew my Mrs. G., of course—and, it turned out, wanted nothing to do with her. After all, she'd gone and "fancied up her name that way...."

Naturally, when they heard about the will it was a different matter. They started legal proceedings instantly.

But Mr. Eldridge was, and had been, a very hardworking lawyer: Mrs. G. had, through him, filed a new will every six months for the last five years of her life, changing a few bequests around the edges but always keeping the same basic provisions. If one will was tossed out of court there was always another one waiting in the wings.

Eventually, the cousins settled for next to nothing. A mere pittance.

Fifty thousand dollars each.

And me?

I got my fee.

I told myself that was all I was going to get and, until the next time (a year and a half later) attorney Eldridge called, I guess I believed it. He didn't call about Mrs. Green; he had another "estate matter" for me to look into, and this one was only seven hundred and fifty thousand dollars. (But—guess what? The will in that one left him a trust fund of one hundred thousand dollars.

There are times when being a lawyer seems worthwhile.)

Over such a comparatively small matter, of course, he came over to my office that time. And we got to chatting. "Remember," he said casually, "I told you we'd get a tax break if Mrs. Greenleaf could be shown to be older than she claimed?"

I remembered.

"Well, a joint committee of Congress reviewed the claim, and we got a rebate. Six hundred and seventy-two thousand dollars. Just thought you'd like to know."

So I stuck out my hand, friendly-like, to shake his—with my palm turned ever so slightly upward. Mr. Eldridge was a smart cookie; he never missed a trick.

He shook my hand.

"The satisfaction of a job well done," he said. "That ought to be enough payment, on a real toughie like the Greenleaf case."

Sure.

Oh, by the way. . . .

Remember Mr. Kozinsky? The guy who got a ten-million-dollar trust out of that estate? Kozinsky was even more unlucky than I have ever been. Six months after Mrs. G. died, he died—and, because the estate hadn't been settled by then, what with the cousins and so on, he never saw a penny of income. By now, either it's gone to the Institute of Physics, or the State of New York's got it—as "abandoned property." I wouldn't know.

So, all in all: as I said, a nice dull case.

A Nice Dull Job

No shootings, no gangsters, no wooden Indians, elecric razors or spies.

Just money.

But . . . what a *lot* of it.

INTERLUDE III

The primary reason why a man runs away from home is money—either not enough of it, or else too much of it.

It's easier to find a person who's been missing ten years than it is to find one who's been missing ten days.

A woman who married a man who says he has absolutely no relatives, who's vague about where he was brought up, where he went to school, where he spent most of his early life—a woman in that spot is in for trouble. Most people have *some* relatives (and everybody has some sort of past history); the reason a man doesn't want to talk about them, or about past events, is that he has something to hide. It may be entirely innocent.

It may not, too.

A close friend of mine, an engineer, has often told me that he's fascinated by what I do for a living. Frankly, I'm fascinated by whatever it is engineers do.

One of our operatives got license plates for his car that read TRACER.
I fired him.

Everyone, to some degree, is an escapist. What it takes to trigger the escape mechanism is what makes one person different from another.

Whenever I help a client set up a "missing person" poster, I insist that there be no offer of reward. The dollar signs seem to affect people's eyesight: pretty soon everybody begins to look like the missing person.

I know a private investigator who's never been out

Interlude III

of New York. But his stationery has the names of the far-flung capitals of the world all around the margin.

13
MONEY, MONEY, WHO WANTS THE MONEY?

As you go along in this business, there are a great many things to learn—and, if you're lucky, you learn a few of them now and then. More than "a few" I can't claim; there always seems to be another small one around the corner, and (to my great relief) the supply doesn't appear to be giving out. It makes matters interesting—which is the way I like them to be, or I'd never have cut out of accountancy in the first place for this slightly nutty trade—let alone have stayed out, all this time.

As for instance . . . well, one case I remember had an odd lesson tagged to it. The rule I got from that one was: When a case is finished—it isn't finished. Some of the time, anyhow. It's awfully easy to come up with an answer to a given problem, but that isn't what the client is paying you for. He doesn't want you to come up with an answer: he wants you to come up with the *right* answer. And, once in a while, you can persuade yourself that the answer you've worked for *is* the right one. In fact, you can be entirely and totally sure.

That, as I found out, is the time to take a deep breath and check everything all over again. Maybe you're right, and the job is done . . . but maybe, just maybe, you've managed to box yourself into a tight corner which, while perfectly lovely to look at, isn't at all the corner you thought you were standing in, or the corner you were supposed to be standing in.

The man who taught me that small lesson wasn't, as it happened, a client at all. He wasn't even the person I was looking for. In a way, he had nothing to do with the case at all. . . .

This one began, like the Greenleaf case, with a lawyer. Mr. Franklyn Clay, an elderly and very proper partner in an elderly and very proper Boston law firm, came down to New York for a talk. Mr. Clay wasn't used to employing private detectives, but he'd naturally heard of Tracers Company and, when every other line of inquiry he could think of had gone dry, he'd come to our offices.

Mr. Clay was trying to give some money away.

Now, as you may have noticed, this is not really an uncommon situation. A fair number of times, when a lawyer is attempting to fulfill the terms of a client's will, he discovers that someone named in it, about to inherit under that will, has moved, changed employers, or just plain becomes difficult to find; after all, between the drawing up of that will and its execution quite a number of years can go by.

Mr. Clay was looking for a man I'll call William McKinnon, last known at an address in Allentown, Pennsylvania. McKinnon, as a cousin of Mr. Clay's late client, was due to inherit a small fraction of the client's estate—the small fraction being a bit over one hundred thousand dollars.

Of course, Mr. Clay hadn't just checked out the address and given up. For one thing, Mrs. McKinnon still lived at that address—though she hadn't seen her husband in five and a half years. Mr. Clay had spent some time writing letters and getting replies from Mrs. McKinnon, but his information seemed a little vague. As far as he knew, Mrs. McKinnon hadn't heard from her husband since he'd walked out of her life five and a half years before. Whether the marriage had ever been legally terminated he couldn't say for sure. "I'm afraid that Mrs. McKinnon is—understandably, I should say—reluctant to discuss the matter," he told me.

It occurred to me that the idea of a hundred thousand dollars might go a long way toward overcoming reluctance, but Mr. Clay was firm on that point: she'd told him very nearly nothing.

I got some further background data from him, and thought for a short while about possible approaches. Finding a missing heir isn't usually the most difficult job

Tracers Company runs into. For one thing, there's no reason to keep the hunt quiet, or to disguise it as some other type of search: the more people who know about the hunt, after all, the better your chances of reaching the heir. And most people seem to feel pretty good about helping another person to some good luck; as a rule, information comes quickly and easily, and the job is about as simple as you can expect anything in this business to be.

There are, of course, exceptions. And Mrs. McKinnon, on the basis of the very few facts I had, sounded like a tougher proposition than usual. After all, she knew of the bequest—and she'd still told the lawyer nothing worth mentioning.

There were, of course, other places to begin, but. . . .

When in doubt, I told myself, try the obvious. Even when things look a little strange, the odds are with you; most moves wouldn't be obvious unless, most of the time, they worked. There was plenty of time for complicated work, if matters came to that—but the obvious came first.

So, since I happened to be less tied up with other jobs at the moment than most of the staff, I packed a bag and headed for Allentown, Pennsylvania.

Mrs. McKinnon, a woman in her late thirties, didn't seem disposed to be cooperative; she insisted, in fact, that I must have had the "whole story from the neighbors," and she wasn't fond of that idea at all. I told her, quite truthfully, that I hadn't spoken to anyone in Allentown before coming to see her. "The whole town knows about it, anyhow," she said. "He got into debt, and he left me; that's all. But it's enough for them to keep on talking about."

I mentioned that the inheritance should take care of the debt problem, in any case, and Mrs. McKinnon, handing me my first small surprise, asked me just how much money was involved.

Mr. Clay, apparently, hadn't thought it necessary either to give her that information, or to tell me he hadn't. She assumed, I discovered, that we'd been talking about two or three hundred dollars. When I told her that her husband—and he was still her husband: Mrs. McKinnon has neither started nor received word of any legal proceedings—was due to come into an inheritance just five hundred times as big as the "two hundred dollars" she hadn't much bothered with, she began to act as if she wanted to tell me something—something she hadn't mentioned to Franklyn Clay.

All she said at first, though, was: "I'm—not sure I know where Bill is. I'm not even sure I could get in touch with him."

That uncertainty was the first piece of good news I'd had. It meant, of course, that Mrs. McKinnon had kept up some sort of communication with her husband; if she hadn't, she wouldn't have been uncertain. She'd have been *sure* she didn't know where he was.

I asked her about that communication.

"Yes," she said, "I've—had a letter or two from him. The last one—well, there were more than one or two. They arrive about once a year. And the last one came from Louisiana, a little place near Baton Rouge."

I asked her for the letter, and she said she didn't have that, but she'd kept the address. It was a place I'll call the Starlite Motel; but, she added when she gave it to me, that wasn't where Bill had been staying. The manager, he'd told her, would hold letters for him, and he'd wanted some personal papers sent on to Walter Molyneaux, at the motel.

"I don't even know if he got the papers," Mrs. McKinnon said. "I haven't heard from him since."

Mrs. McKinnon gave me a description of her husband, though she had no pictures. He had black hair, gray eyes, no distinguishing marks; he was five feet ten and weighed a hundred and eighty-five pounds—all that of course, as of five and a half years before. He had been about forty-five when he'd left; he'd be about fifty now, she said.

He'd been a CPA and was considered something of a mathematical wizard. He'd belonged to an Allentown bridge club and had been thought of as an expert player. Outside of bridge, his only hobbies were fishing and reading.

None of his letters, his wife said, had had any return address that he'd admitted had been his residence.

I told her, when I had all that straight, that we'd do our best to find her husband. She looked at me as if she didn't believe a word I said.

The Starlite Motel had an owner-manager—whose name, to my slight surprise, didn't turn out to be Walter Molyneaux. Hal Boyer, though, did give me a good lead toward Molyneaux: he'd hired a man of that name as an accountant for a while, but had dropped him because he was "real handy with figures—a little too handy, if you see what I mean. In fact, the guy was a crook."

"A crook?" I said.

Hal Boyer shrugged. "Makes out two tax returns, you know? One for the sucker, one for the government. And you know who gets the spread."

Boyer gave me the names of several other people Molyneaux had worked for, and told me that as far as he knew Molyneaux was living on a houseboat tied up in a nearby bayou. "The guy likes to fish," he said.

All right: that much checked out. A description of McKinnon, Boyer told me, fit Molyneaux to a T. As I'd begun to suspect before leaving Allentown, McKinnon and Molyneaux appeared to be turning out to be one person.

Most people who take a false name do tend to keep their own initials; there are a good many explanations for this, some of them psychological (the person really wants to be found, for instance—which is sometimes, if by no means always, true) and some just practical (if you've got luggage, or clothing, or other personal items already initialled, it may seem simpler to hang on to the initials while changing the rest of the name). Given William McKinnon and Walter Molyneaux—both accountants—fitting the same description—with the same hobby—and with the same initials—I thought my search was just about over.

I'd reached the end of the case.

Unfortunately, this didn't happen to be true.

Molyneaux wasn't too hard to find. On the way to locating just which houseboat in just which bayou he was living in, I talked to other people who'd hired him. Boyer's assessment of the man as a crook didn't agree with anything the others said or implied, but he was, at least, right about the houseboat. There was one, hidden away in the bends of a swamp. A girl who said she knew Molyneaux (and who was suspicious of me even after I'd tried to prove to her that I was carrying no warrant and wasn't there to arrest anyone) took me out.

Molyneaux fit the description, all right. And, he told me, he was very much interested in the hundred thousand dollars.

But, he went on, he wasn't William McKinnon. McKinnon had met him in a bar more than a year before, and since McKinnon was broke Molyneaux let him stay in Molyneaux' room at the Starlite Motel, and even receive mail under the Molyneaux name.

Where was McKinnon now? "Maybe New Orleans," Molyneaux said. "He always talked about going down there. Say—is there a reward for finding this guy?"

There wasn't, as far as I knew; but Molyneaux cheered up anyhow. "When this guy gets his money," he said, "you might tell him I helped to spot him. Maybe he'll need a CPA to handle his income taxes for him."

Which was pretty funny—but which left me with all the job still to do, and very few leads of any kind.

Boyer, back at the Starlite Motel, confirmed that Molyneaux had shared his cabin with someone else, but claimed never to have seen the other person. Nobody around Baton Rouge had seen anyone answering McKinnon's description—except, of course, for such identifications as checked right back to Molyneaux. Molyneaux had been helpful, I kept telling myself; but every time one of those descriptions checked back he got easier and easier to dislike.

After two days of checking there, I followed the only lead I seemed to have, and went on to New Orleans.

Meanwhile, centering on New Orleans, we'd started a large canvassing operation.

Employment bureaus were told of the search and a description was furnished to each one, on what seemed the fair chance that McKinnon was using a different name. A check of every bridge club in New Orleans was begun. An ad in newspaper personals columns offered a reward.

I did a lot of the canvassing myself, and it was the sort of routine that sounds almost as boring as it actually is: you ask the same questions time after time and day after day of an endless parade of people; you try patiently to jog memories; you find out that, regarding the case you're interested in, there are no memories to jog. And then you start all over again.

There's only one thing that makes it all worth doing: the chance that *this* man, *this* place *this* question, will suddenly open the case up for you. It can happen any time—and my knowledge of that fact helps keep boredom at a reasonable distance. For a while, at any rate.

After three weeks, though, it had begun to creep up on me; we were, in fact, almost ready to conclude that McKinnon was nowhere near New Orleans at all, no matter what he'd said or what Molyneaux had thought.

It was a bridge player, though, who did open up the case for us, before we finally decided to shut up shop. He was a little, elderly man named Hedley. He told me he'd seen McKinnon here and there and even played bridge with him in a New Orleans park where McKinnon had been a "regular" for a while. It had all been two or three years ago, he thought, but he was sure he had the right man.

After all, he went on, it isn't every day you discover that your ex-bridge partner is wanted for embezzlement and grand larceny.

Hedley hadn't found that fact out until McKinnon was gone from his usual seat in the park; he'd happened on his partner's face staring at him out of a Wanted poster in a post office display, and he'd taken the poster down and kept it ever since.

That, as far as Tracers Company was concerned, finished the case. William McKinnon had been a fugitive from justice for five and a half years: his debts had gotten a bit too much for him, and he'd embezzled money from the company he worked for. I sent Mr. Clay (the lawyer who'd hired us, away back in New York) a full report, suggesting that the inheritance gave McKinnon a chance to pay back the money he'd taken —if he ever turned up. But the police had spent five and a half years looking for him and, officially, had the case still open. Our own official responsibility stopped right there.

After thinking things over a bit, though, I asked Hedley to give me the Wanted poster, and I mailed it off to McKinnon, suggesting that we meet in New Orleans and talk matters over.

He phoned me two days later, and set up a meeting for a deserted part of town at eleven that night. When we met, he told me that he'd once tried to talk to the company from which he'd embezzled about paying back the money, and that they wouldn't hear of it under any circumstances; at fifty, he said to me, he wasn't about to head for prison, not even for one hundred thousand dollars. If I informed the police, that was my business; he was shipping out, next morning, to an extradition-free country.

After all, he wound up, if I'd found him—then maybe the police could, too. He was taking no more chances.

McKinnon?

Well, that's what I meant, when I said that sometimes, when a case is over—it isn't over.

McKinnon, obviously, was Walter Molyneaux.

Everything really *had* added up, regardless of what "Molyneaux" had told me. True, some fairly wild coincidences do happen—but that one seemed a bit too much. When I added it to the fact that people had seen and talked to Molyneaux in Baton Rouge, while no one had seen McKinnon under any other name, the set of coincidences kept me worrying through three weeks of work in New Orleans.

The Wanted poster, as I said, opened up the case.

If Molyneaux was McKinnon, he had to have a pretty strong reason for turning his back on one hundred thousand dollars. Nothing in the case had given me any hint of that reason—until Hedley came up with it. Once Molyneaux' motive for refusing to admit he was McKinnon came clear, the chain of coincidence became a chain of evidence instead.

(Oh—that person rooming with Molyneaux at the Starlite Motel? I asked him about that, in New Orleans. That person was the girl who'd so suspiciously guided me to the Molyneaux houseboat.)

Where McKinnon is now, I have no idea. That case, I suppose, has to be left just a little bit up in the air.

But there is one more fact. I asked McKinnon how much he'd embezzled, and he told me.

He'd stolen six thousand dollars.

In order to avoid prison, he had to turn his back on almost twenty times that amount.

Crime, as they say, doesn't pay.

14
THE REALLY EVIL PEOPLE

Tracers Company of America is, as you'll have seen by this time, hired to hunt down a good many different kinds of people, every week of every month. There are men who run out on their wives and wives who run out on their husbands. There are teen-agers leaving home. There are debtors skipping out on their obligations. There are con men, too, taking off after a successful "score" with their neatly gotten gains.

None of those, though, is the type I dislike most. For me, the really reprehensible characters—the really evil people—come up for action all too frequently. These are the "technical kidnappers."

What I mean by the term is the parent of a child who, after having been separated or divorced from his/her spouse and then denied full or partial custody of the child (or, of course, children), moves against that court ruling and actually "kidnaps" his own child.

There are, of course, people who tell me that an act like that might be considered a show of the love felt by the parent for the child. It's an interesting theory. Who knows? I might even agree with it—if it weren't for one thing.

I've run into a few facts. Mostly, those facts have to do with what takes place *after* the kidnapping.

In what I'll call the Brown case, as it happens, there was no divorce to begin with, and no court ruling for the "kidnapper" to defy; but the "technical kidnapping" itself is, I'm afraid, about typical of the way this sort of thing does run, and the case has, as well, a few special features.

The background is rather lengthy; I'll give it the way Philip Brown (as I'll call him) gave it to me, condensed as far as possible and, as far as possible, made simply a parade of facts instead of a good part of the story of several lives.

Philip Brown, an electrical engineer, met Eleanor Neilson in Los Angeles and, after a whirlwind courtship, married her. Their honeymoon trip took them to Fairbanks, Alaska, where Philip's new job was supposed to start two weeks later.

At first, everything was wonderful. Eleanor, who like most of us had never been to Alaska, was fascinated by her first visit to the town and the people, and all the novelty of actually being a wife, just like in the TV shows and soap operas, kept things in a rosy glow for her.

The rosy glow, though, didn't last long. Fairbanks is neither as warm nor, for an electrical engineer and family, as luxurious as Southern California; Eleanor took to calling the place "the wildnerness," and in other ways as well her irritation started to show. It wasn't due only to the cold and the lack of a few luxuries, either.

In the first place, she was pregnant, due to have a baby the following January, and morning sickness didn't make her days any more pleasant. Too, she'd had a pile of friends in Los Angeles, and had spent a good deal of time out on those Southern California beaches, surrounded by people she knew and liked; in Fairbanks she was alone most of the time, and she began to feel very much "out of things." A vicious circle started: the more "out of things" she felt, the more irritable she became; as her anger and unhappiness increased, she withdrew more and more into herself; and the more withdrew, the more "out of things" she was.

The solid promises of steady work and promotions from the company Philip worked for meant less than nothing after a bit; she was not going to stay in Fairbanks any longer; she wanted out!

Philip, faced with this, felt that he ought to keep his bride reasonably happy. What's more, she'd managed to convince him that Alaska was no place to bring up an infant. He therefore tried to get a transfer to a California office of the same company.

The transfer was refused—and Philip resigned.

Back in California (where they immediately moved—right on back to L.A., in fact), he somehow couldn't manage to make a connection. Time was passing. Nobody was getting much happier: his bank account, saved before his marriage, was going fast, and what he'd managed to add to that account while in Fairbanks was going, it seemed, even faster. Philip's parents were dead, and he'd gotten used to being self-reliant: When he broached the subject of parents, Eleanor told him that her own mother and father were back East, "and anyhow, they're not my own parents—and I wouldn't go to them for help if I were starving, let me tell you." Eleanor, it developed, had been an adopted child, and she'd lit out for the West Coast on her own two years before, grabbing a job as athletic director for a day school; the job didn't pay much but it did give her a good chance for many long hours on those beaches, and every once in a while, as a dividend, a weekend ski trip.

Philip's only living relative was a sister, in Chicago. She had three children of her own, and was certainly in no position to help Philip out until he could make some new connection for work in his field.

So, he grabbed the first job he could find—as a department-store floorwalker. At least, he told himself, it brought in some money; and, for a time, the marriage appeared to be settling down, becoming comparatively peaceful. The Browns' first baby was born, and matters became worse only very slowly.

But they did, of course, become worse.

Philip's own career was, naturally enough, part of the trouble. A trained electrical engineer, he was in no shape to stand around a department store all day, cooped up in a job he didn't understand or like, and, careerwise, going nowhere fast.

It got on his nerves, to put it mildly. And so did Eleanor's strange new attitude: she seemed almost to ignore him, forget he was anywhere around. She seemed to devote herself entirely to the baby. Philip began to wonder if an attention switch that sudden, and that total, was normal. . . .

Slowly, too, he found himself taking days off (calling in "sick") to make sure the baby was really cared for. Eleanor paid attention to nothing else—but the attention she paid the baby didn't extend much to practical details. She just gave up at the sight of a pile of dirty diapers. A trip to the laundromat exhausted her. The two o'clock feeding exhausted her, too . . . and Philip made the gradual discovery that, if he didn't take care of the baby, the baby wouldn't be taken care of.

Obviously the situation was getting worse and worse. But . . . what else was there for him to do?

He found out, a year after the move back to Los Angeles, when he ran into an old classmate, and got to talking, and found himself with a job offer in his own specialty. It wasn't a job in Los Angeles, or even in the United States. It meant South America, he told Eleanor, but: "It's warm there," he added. "Like California. No more snow-and-ice stuff; you'll like it fine down there."

Eleanor was in the second month of her second pregnancy.

If Philip had any forebodings, he kept them to himself. Eleanor seemed happy; the company in South America liked his work. His blocked life seemed, suddenly, to have opened up again.

Then, six months after the South American move, Elenor took the children and disappeared.

Philip was frantic. South American police turned up nothing helpful. He flew to L.A.—and again found nothing.

A month of this sort of harried searching went on before Philip, back at work, got a call from Eleanor's adoptive father, Sam Neilson, in New York. Eleanor and the children had been there. She had refused even to discuss returning to South America, and the prospect of a coming New York winter (it was then late August, but she was looking ahead) seemed too much for her as well.

So she'd left again—and had just called Sam Neilson. From Tucson, Arizona.

Philip asked for, and got, the address and telephone number his wife was using there. Then he called her.

He told her he was willing to give up the South American job, tie up all the loose ends and meet her in Tucson within a week or two—to try once more to make some sense out of their marriage.

She sounded as if she accepted the idea, but when he arrived in Tucson and called her again, a woman who said she was the landlady of the apartment answered the phone. Eleanor and the children had left the week before. She had no idea where they might have gone.

Philip spent one solid year trying to find her and the children. He tried the police, and he tried doing some tracking on his own. At the end of the year, he showed up in my office and told me, essentially, what I've just written down.

For me, of course, the first thing was a call to Sam Neilson and his wife—checking to make sure they had not heard from Eleanor since the Tucson call the year before. Once that was thoroughly out of the way, I began to dig around in the obvious places. Once again, the rule came in handy: looking for a runaway, begin by checking his back trail. Just to see if, maybe, he (or in this case she) had dropped a clue or two in the rush to get started.

There just wasn't any other place to look.

Eleanor (I learned) had gotten a job within a week after her arrival in Tucson. She was a clerk at a private day school. It meant no more than office work, filing and a little typing, and nobody was really terribly perturbed when she left on one day's notice. The only additional fact that turned up when I started sifting through that stretch of Eleanor's history was that the girls' gym teacher had left on the same day.

Coincidence? Maybe. Then again, maybe not; and the only way to find out was to ask some more questions.

I talked with two other teachers, and over the

course of some long and mostly irrelevant conversations a picture began to emerge. It wasn't really a very pretty picture.

In something under three weeks, Eleanor and the gym teacher, a girl I'll call Janet, had become the closest of friends. Janet had previously kept everyone else, male and female, at arm's length, but Eleanor seemed to be different. "They acted like—" one of the teachers began, and finally finished by grimly saying the word: "Well, like a couple of—of lesbians."

The statement was loaded, as delivered, not only with embarrassment but with spite. I have no idea why —and until and unless a case comes up in which it might be important, I don't much care why. But the statement had been made.

All right. There were, as I knew, cases on record— quite a number of them—of lesbians who made a determined effort to suppress their own tendencies, who married, bore children, and then, finally unable to stand the life they'd made for themselves, chucked it all and struck out for new land and pleasanter dreams. If Eleanor was one such case, I had a lead: find Janet, and the odds were I'd find Eleanor as well.

And if she weren't. . . .

Well, then, I'd think of something else. The principle looks like this: find an opening. If necessary, invent one (and it sometimes is necesssary). See where it leads. And if it leads nowhere—why, then, go on back and find (or invent) another opening.

That time, though, the job was reasonably simple. Janet was an accredited teacher, originally from Boston.

A little checking there turned up hospital records: she'd had a thoracic operation a year before she'd finished college, and the surgeon had suggested her going to a warm, dry climate—like Arizona. She'd been in Tucson for five years, and out of touch with her family (still in Boston) for four; in fact, the family asked me to notify them if I found out that she was all right—which, eventually, I was able to do.

In other words, I'd tracked Janet from college to Tucson. In terms of the problem, I knew almost exactly what I'd known before. Except for one thing, mentioned casually: Janet had liked skiing, her parents said.

Eleanor had liked it, too. It began to look as if I was in for a long routine, checking the various ski areas of the country. I began to settle down with the beginnings of that interminable job. . . .

Sometimes, someone else does your work for you. The teacher who'd given me the word on Eleanor's friendship with Janet called me, collect, from Tucson.

She'd noticed an application form on a school office desk: Janet's, applying for a job in a Maine school. She gave me the name of the school district, and that of the local superintendent. She thought I might be interested.

I was. I was also grateful; my secretary dropped over to Saks Fifth Avenue later that day and picked out a good and expensive perfume, which I sent right on to that Tucson schoolteacher.

Meanwhile, I took a deep breath and put on my very best M.D. voice. I convinced a Maine superintendent of schools that I was the surgeon who'd done the thoracic job on Janet—not too difficult, since I had all the data on the operation.

"You see, I understood she was beginning a teaching job in your district," I said, "and I—"

"Why—is there anything wrong with her, Doctor?" he asked me. "After all, we need a gym teacher, and if she isn't capable of fulfilling her duties—"

"No, no, nothing like that," I said. "No need to worry. I simply wondered why she hadn't stopped by on her way up there to see me, as she had said she would. I would like an examination, yes—but there's no reason to feel that the results would show anything to hamper her activity in any way."

The superintendent, naturally enough, suggested notifying Janet I was looking for her, and having her give me a call. I had to avoid that one:

"Frankly, I wish you wouldn't: she might get alarmed, for no reason—but you know how people are. A message from a doctor . . . well, it's really nothing that need be rushed. Why not just give me the telephone number and the address—I might just drop her a note, after all."

I made it sound casual enough, and I got my information.

At that point, I called Philip Brown (who was staying with his sister's family in Chicago) and told him to stand by.

From New York to a small town a couple of miles this side of the Canadian border was a trip by cab, plane and hired car, and it put me a quarter of a mile from the address the superintendent had given me, more or less, by noon the next day—right in front of a combination gas station and grocery store. (Which has always struck me as a good arrangement, by the way. Saves time.) I asked a young man at the gas pump there where my address was—mentioning casually that I understood the place was for rent the rest of the season (and "season" was right: it was a ski town, too; some days you can't do anything wrong) and I wanted to go take a look at it.

"Rent?" he said. "I didn't know Ellie and Jan and the kids were leaving. Heck, they better pay me last month's bill before they go."

And that, of course, did it. I was back in a plane shortly, and stopped over in Boston by 5 P.M. Drove from there into Worcester. My mother has learned to expect me to pop in every once in a while, unannounced; besides, she thinks I'm undernourished, and takes every chance she can find to feed me up a little. I'm six feet tall. I weigh two hundred pounds.

I'd called Philip Brown, given him the name and number of a deputy sheriff up there, and waited for news. Philip called me in my New York office early the next morning to describe the scene to me. . . .

He'd arranged to meet the deputy at Presque Isle airport, Maine, and to have a small plane standing by there. About two in the afternoon, Philip and the deputy, in a rented car, pulled up in front of the house.

The deputy flashed his badge and demanded to be let in; Janet, who'd opened the door, tried to slam it in his face. The deputy, with Philip's aid, forced it back open—just in time to catch Eleanor trying to swoop both kids up in her arms and get out the back door with them.

The Deputy grabbed the older child. Philip reached for the baby—and found himself literally involved in a tug-o'-war. The baby was the rope.

There was screaming and swearing, and a long and vicious fight; nobody got out undamaged—but at last they did get out, and Philip took the children on to Chicago.

The kids, he told me, were going to a doctor that afternoon, for a general checkup. After the fight, it was clear that they needed one.

So: Eleanor Brown tried to duck her own problem, using Philip and then the children as shields—and failed. Philip tried to make the marriage work, and kept on trying to do that by ignoring the facts—and failed.

But those two kids—what did they try?

What had they done—to be yanked around, battered, screamed over, bruised . . . ?

15
ONE IN A MILLION

There's a newspaper story the reporters seem to keep on ice for days when very little is happening. It's always just about the same, and the only major changes are the name and the amount. It reports that so-and-so, a shabby and obviously moneyless recluse, died the day before, and has been found to have savings of such-and-such millions of dollars. For some reason, the bankbooks showing the amount are always sewn into his overcoat, or his underwear. It sounds like an uncomfortable way to carry bankbooks, but who am I to argue with a millionaire? Especially a shabby, obviously moneyless, reclusive millionaire.

As I say, that one pops up every so often. A couple of detective stories and, weirdly enough, at least one science-fiction story have been based on it. I have no idea what the odds are on its being a true story in any given instance—I mean, *some* of the skid row characters must really be broke—but if I had to give a quotation I'd call it at one shot in a million.

Naturally, Tracers Company ran into that one—the deceased recluse with the pile of money. It was only twenty thousand dollars, but along skid row that's about the same as a million.

Naturally too, when we ran into it we ran into a full set of oddities connected to the case. We had a client: the recluse's brother, who hadn't seen him in years, and hadn't tried to find him. We had the recluse himself: dead of a heart attack after some cheerful teen-age hoodlum—apparently having heard a rumor about the money, and determined to get to the bottom of things—had beaten him unconscious.

What we didn't have was the money.

At first, of course, I suspected there wasn't any. (No bankbooks in the overcoat or the underwear. In fact, no bankbooks anyplace. Clearly the case wasn't going according to form.) But the brother was, he told us, absolutely sure.

There was twenty thousand dollars lying around somewhere. The brother didn't know where, the recluse couldn't tell, and (the police told us) there'd been no sudden oddity in spending patterns around this particular skid row, which was in Boston. So the teen-age hood hadn't found the money either.

Neither had the police.

Of course, there were no bankbooks, and no obvious clues. In fact, it looked as if there was just about nothing at all.

Clearly, it was a typical Tracers Company job: nice and simple. Just as easy, I told myself, as rolling off an alligator.

I started with some history. About thirty years before, Michael Krikorian had turned up in Boston. He'd been poor and, apparently, friendless: his brother had changed his name to John Gregory; Gregory had apparently reached this country first, from the Krikorians' native Armenia, and had given Michael no help whatever.

Michael had been poking around in trash cans in Boston parks, and was more or less of a familiar figure in such circles as gather around trash cans; that, as far as anyone knew, had been his sole occupation for thirty years. (When I was told that he'd managed to accumulate twenty thousand dollars in that time, I began wondering what people throw away in Boston.) The police picked up the teen-ager who'd beaten him, and they poked around in Michael's rooms—he'd lived in a small, cluttered place rented out by a Mrs. Palamas, along with a good many other, and less affluent, characters.

The room had given the police their only clue to the money—which, in any case, was not their concern. They found a slip of paper in what Mrs. Palamas said was Michael's handwriting. The slip of paper had $20,000 written on it.

That, when we began, was that. As far as Michael was concerned.

His brother, John Gregory, had come to the U.S. as an immigrant, too, and had prospered. In fact, he was an officer of the Commonwealth Bank, also in Boston but about as far away from Michael's living quarters as it was possible to get and still be in the same city. He hadn't known, in any sort of detail, how his brother was making out; in fact, it was police research that turned him up. That, combined with newspaper stories about the millionaire recluse.

It was very unlikely that police search of Michael's rooms had left a stone or so unturned. But there was nothing except the unlikely to start with, so I went on to Boston and found Mrs. Palamas' rooming house.

Mrs. Palamas was a large, overweight woman who was sure of only one thing: there wasn't any money. "Anybody got twenty thousand dollars," she told me, "he don't live in this place." I could see the point: the room was small and dirty and somehow hopeless. It was being kept open: John Gregory had insisted on that. Michael Krikorian had paid two weeks' rent in advance, and for two weeks nobody was to enter the room except the police and the investigator John had hired: me. Mrs. Palamas didn't much like the idea—she could have rented the place ten times over, she told me—but she obeyed it.

I went through the room as carefully as possible, for a while. There were some newspapers in Armenian. There was a souvenir postcard of the Statue of Liberty. Somehow this didn't seem to get me anywhere. I remember that I'd just picked up a small green elephant—a paperweight-size piece of colored glass—when a man at the open door of the room asked me what I was doing.

I put the elephant down and turned around. The man's name, I found out quickly enough, was Smurda. He was a tall, thin fellow in his sixties who thought of himself as "the Poet Laureate of the slums," and for all I know he was.

I told him I was an investigator, and asked if he had known Krikorian. He said he did. He also said he knew John Gregory—Gregory, it seemed, had already been by, asking about the money.

"What did you tell him?" I said.

Smurda gave me a gigantic, ultrapoetic shrug—"I don't know about such things," he said. "Thirty years ago, Michael came to this country. His brother refused to sponsor his visa. Michael never forgot."

Whether he really knew nothing about the money, or just disliked Gregory, I couldn't tell. There wasn't any immediate way of finding out, but I thought I might get a little more from him than the background I'd already had from Gregory. We talked for a long while. He told me, in fact, that Michael resented his brother's having refused sponsorship: "Like that green elephant you were holding," Smurda said, "he forgot nothing." Whether this was true or not, I didn't know. Smurda clearly had the not unusual habit of assuming that everyone he knew shared his attitudes toward anything he talked about.

But he did say that, once a week, Michael Krikorian had gone to another part of the city.

But that was all. "Another part of the city" left us a lot of room.

I reported as much to Gregory, and asked, as what was very nearly a last-chance query, who *had* sponsored Michael's arrival in the U.S. He gave me the name of a wealthy man in Back Bay, and even though the event was thirty years old he dug up that name and address very quickly. Apparently he'd been keeping a file on Michael.

The question was, obviously: had Michael Krikorian told anyone where he'd kept the money?

The further question—whether or not there was any money—was beginning to fade out. The only disbeliever was Mrs. Palamas; by the time I was heading for Back Bay, even I was feeling pretty well convinced.

Still, I'd have liked some evidence....

The Back Bay address turned out to be a large house, still tenanted. The man who'd sponsored Michael Krikorian had died eight years ago, but his granddaughter knew the story and gave it to me without much hesitation when I explained what I was trying to do. (By that time, the story had really begun to hit the newspapers; banks and such were being circularized with an artist's sketch of Krikorian in the shapeless overcoat he never seemed to leave behind; the woman in Back

Bay knew of the case—unless she'd been deaf, dumb and blind she could hardly have helped knowing.)

Krikorian had tried to enter the country twice—illegally. After the second try had been reported in the Boston papers, the old man had seen the story and determined that anyone who wanted to come here badly enough to keep trying ought to have his chance.

Unfortunately, there had been no mention of money, beyond the fact that the old man had enough to serve as a sponsor. Michael Krikorian, according to the granddaughter, never looked as if he had money; I got the same description from her that I was getting from everyone who'd seen him, complete with overcoat.

Well, I told myself, if there was no faster way of doing it, there was always the old routine. There was always the asking of questions, ten times, twenty times, fifty times . . . the same questions, over and over again.

Sooner or later, I told myself, routine would pay off.

I tried very hard to believe it.

Krikorian had gone somewhere once a week. He'd started from Mrs. Palamas' rooming house, and he hadn't traveled by taxi—someone would certainly have notice that.

Given the location of the rooming house, there were only a few bus lines to try. The bus lines involved quite a number of drivers, but I was lucky: I think it was the twelfth one I tried who remembered Krikorian. "The old coot in the heavy overcoat," he said, and told me how, every Wednesday, Krikorian had got on, taken a transfer to another bus line, and climbed off at the corner that served as intersection point for the lines. Later the same day, the driver said, Krikorian would climb on at the corner, and ride home.

Wonderful. I now had a whole new army of bus drivers to question.

I went to the intersection point, and started off. That time I ran into real luck: the second man I talked to was the driver I wanted. When it happens like that, even the dullest routine doesn't seem so bad.

I got on the bus and got off where, according to the driver, Krikorian had. There was a bank on the corner.

Unfortunately, nobody in the bank had ever heard of Krikorian, or remembered seeing him.

Well, you can't win them all.

But I was a little ahead, at least. If Michael Krikorian had gone to the same corner every week, he'd been heading someplace—someplace in particular. And in this new section of town he was going to stand out. He'd have been noticed.

I started asking people: store managers, newsboys and the like. They'd seen him, all right. I was able to follow his tracks for several blocks and around a corner or two before I got to the Armenian-American Social Hall.

And that, in a strange sort of way, was the jackpot.

That, and a six-year-old boy.

The secretary of the Armenian-American Club which used the hall told me that Krikorian had come around every week to visit a man named Artin Narak. Narak was away at the time, but if I liked he'd send someone down with me to talk to his wife. I told him he just had to give me the address, but he insisted, and told me why: Mrs. Narak spoke no English.

I don't speak Armenian. I collected a combination interpreter-chaperone-guide, and we set off.

Through the interpreter, Mrs. Narak told me that she was immensely grateful to Krikorian. He'd sponsored the immigration of her husband and herself, as well as the small boy who'd managed to be born just under the wire in the U.S. In fact, the Naraks had named the boy Michael, after their benefactor.

"If he sponsored you," I said, "he must have had money. Do you know anything about that?"

Mrs. Narak was very sad about disappointing me, but she didn't know a thing. Krikorian was a fine man—he still came to visit once a week, though in recent weeks he had not been around, and if there were something wrong she'd be glad to do what she could, and Artin, she was sure, would do anything he could for such a fine man, who had helped them all so much—and in the meantime didn't I think his namesake was a fine boy?

The namesake—six-year-old Mike Narak—wandered in from another room when his mother called him. He was holding a small green elephant he had been playing with.

I asked him where he had gotten the elephant.

"Mr. Krikorian gave it to me," he said.

Then I did what only the interruption of Smurda, the Poet Laureate of the slums, had kept me from doing back in Krikorian's rooms.

I took a look at the elephant.

The fact I needed was stamped on the underside. It was a free souvenir paperweight given away by a bank.

By—and the coincidence strikes me as exactly fitting—the Commonwealth Bank.

The bank of which John Gregory was an officer.

The rest of it was simple. Krikorian had rented a safety-deposit box there. Nobody had recognized his picture; the bank was the one place he went to in what amounted to a disguise: without his overcoat. And nobody in the bank—a fairly large one—had connected the names Gregory and Krikorian.

Of course, it would take a court order to open the box, and John Gregory was ready to get busy on that at once. I imagine he finally did get the box opened, and take a look at Michael Krikorian's twenty thousand dollars.

But before he did I told him one more thing. Armed with all the data, I'd gone back to talk to Smurda (and to check on that elephant, just to find out for sure that I'd seen the same one in the hands of little Mike). And Smurda had told me about Michael Krikorians's will, which he'd witnessed.

The will was in the safety-deposit box, too. And it left all of Michael Krikorian's money to his godson—Michael Narak.

Smurda got a lot of satisfaction out of that.

Me? Well, I got the satisfaction of a tough job completed, and Tracers Company got the fee.

And John Gregory got—I know, because I gave it to him—one small green elephant.

INTERLUDE IV

I once received this letter from a man: "So please find out exactly when I was born and where, so my wife's family will stop calling me that name."

To dramatize the fact that there is a lot of money lying around unclaimed, I used to say that it totalled five billion dollars. A reporter with the *Wall Street Journal* wanted to write a story about it, and said the figure sounded much too high. Before writing the article, he got to work and found the actual number. It turned out to be fifteen billion dollars.

Nearly every wife whose husband has run away tells me that she can't understand why he did it. After spending five or ten minutes with some of them, though, I do.

On a radio show recently, I was asked the primary reasons why husbands and wives run away. I mentioned, among other items, the meddling mother-in-law. For the next hour, the station's switchboard was lighted up with calls from mothers-in-law. Each of them said substantially the same thing: they don't meddle. It's just that their sons or daughters-in-law need some shaping up.

Of course, from time to time, I'm tempted to run away too . . . but I'm afraid I might be successful.

Once I located a member of the Communist Party in America, to tell him he had inherited five thousand dollars worth of stock from a deceased uncle. The Communist called his uncle a dirty capitalist . . . but he took the money.

Just about every detective story on TV, in the movies and in books seems to involve a missing person problem.

Most men who run away *want* to be found. They just want to know they've been missed. One man actually called me in advance and told me he was going. "If my wife doesn't bother looking for me," he said, "forget you heard from me. But, if she *does* call you, wait a day or two and then come get me. I'll be staying at Grossinger's in the Catskills."

It's finally here . . . I saw an ad in the newspaper the other day soliciting members for a group called, "Escape Unlimited."

16
I'LL COME BACK FOR YOU

The letter said:
"Dear Sir: I have been reading about your work in a magazine and I would like to know if there is anything you can do for me. Back in 1953, due to the death of my husband in Korea, I was unable to care for my little girl, Claudia, and I was forced to place her in an orphanage. About four years later, I remarried. My husband is a very wonderful man and has done everything possible to try to locate my daughter. Unfortunately, we have been unable to find any trace of her and the orphanage will not tell us where she is or who has her. . . ."

Every year Tracers Company receives many letters

from people who, as children, were placed in orphanages or with child adoption agencies or were simply "given away" to friends or strangers. When they grow up, these people become obsessed with the need to find their "real" parents and go to great lengths in their quest.

It is relatively rare, however, for a request to come from a *mother* who, after having placed her child for legal adoption, wants to track the *child* down. Perhaps the original reason for the abandonment is so overpowering that it makes a change of mind inconceivable later. Or perhaps the mother harbors a deep sense of shame and guilt over the adoption in the first place, and cannot face the prospect of confronting her child.

So, when the letter came from Mrs. Muriel Squires (who was Muriel Fuller, until she remarried), I was especially interested—in the rarity.

The letter went on to tell how Muriel Fuller had taken Claudia to the orphanage in Utica, N.Y.; how she had turned the eight-year-old child over to Mrs. Payton, the director; and how, regretfully, she had signed the adoption consent form. Her final words to little Claudia, who had started to cry, were: "It's only for a little while, my darling. Then I'll come back for you."

Mrs. Squires described Claudia as blonde and blue-eyed. More than twelve years had passed since her mother had given her up.

As a child, Claudia had shown outstanding musical talents, and the periodic reports from the orphanage, which were discontinued when Claudia was adopted, told that Claudia's abilities were being recognized and she was being given voice lessons. The orphange was the

Payton Home for Children.

There were no other leads.

I called Mrs. Squires and told her of the extreme difficulties involved in pursuing a search of this sort. I pointed out that no reputable adoption agency would divulge the names of the adopting parents or anything else about the child's circumstances. Even the court record regarding the adoption would be sealed, and a new birth certificate issued for the adopted child.

But, when I heard the voice of Mrs. Squires telling me that she could not retain her sanity until she at least made a final attempt to find her daughter. . . .

Reluctantly, I told her that I would do what I could, but that she should not have very high hopes.

Even though I felt it would probably do no good, I went to Utica and looked up the Payton Home for Children. Mrs. Payton gave me the stock statement: "I assure you, I can fully understand Mrs. Squires' feelings; but she's not the only person to be considered."

I parried with, "Claudia's grown up by now. I can't see that it would do her any harm. She knows she was adopted."

Mrs. Payton quickly pointed out that the adoptive parents might not quite agree with me, but I pressed on. "Has anyone asked the girl?"

"It so happens, Mr. Goldfader, that Claudia *was* consulted several years ago, when Mrs. Squires first made inquiries. But she made it very clear that she had no desire to see her mother."

"Why?" I asked.

"I don't know. Maybe she's resentful over having been abandoned."

So I tried another tack. "Mrs. Squires is now in a position to give her daughter advantages she might not have."

Then Mrs. Payton inadvertently gave me the clue I was looking for: "Claudia's needs are more than adequately taken care of. In addition, I understand she has a career of her own . . . but I'm afraid I can tell you nothing more. A man in your business should know how these things are." She took a deep breath and added: "You never should have come to see me. In my opinion, the whole matter ought to be dropped immediately."

"Mrs. Payton," I said, "I'm with you." And I left.

The reference to the fact that Claudia had a career suggested to me the possibility that the girl had developed her musical abilities and might be singing professionally. (At the same time, of course, I realized that her career might be in any one of a thousand other fields. But singers are easier to trace.)

So, I called my office in New York and instructed that a search of musician's union files be made for a female vocalist, first name Claudia; age about twenty; blonde hair; blue eyes. I told my secretary I would call back in an hour, and I had myself a leisurely lunch.

My secretary gave me the news when I called back: Claudia Montaine, Chicago; Claudia Ellis, with Joe

Rubin's orchestra, currently playing one-night stands in the midwest; and Claudia Blair, the Red Room, Los Angeles.

Chicago was the nearest. If I was lucky, Joe Rubin and his band might not be too far from there either. I just *knew,* all the time, that if one of them was Mrs. Squires' daughter, it would be the one in Los Angeles. Somehow, things always work that way.

I headed for Chicago. You have to go through the motions.

The place where Claudia Montaine was singing was small: the sort of nightclub that hired entertainers who didn't mind working close to the customers. I could almost have reached out to touch the stage from a seat at the bar.

I noted that the singer was blonde, experienced, and very deliberately sexy. But she did fit the general description.

She finished her song. Nobody seemed to notice. She took a bow anyhow, and walked across the dance floor toward the back of the room.

I caught up with her. "Got a minute, Miss Montaine?"

"Sorry. I never drink with the customers."

"This is business."

"I'll bet."

"I'm trying to locate a woman," I told her in my most impersonal voice.

"I know," she said, "things are tough all over."

I ignored that. "She's a singer. Her name is Claudia. She's blonde and has blue eyes. She was adopted twelve years ago. Her natural mother wants to see her again."

"Gee," she said, "that's heartrending."

"How about it, Miss Montaine?"

"I'll ask the old lady next time I see her. If I *was* adopted, she'd have given me back long ago."

"Doesn't prove anything." (I couldn't resist.) "Maybe she tried." (And I ducked, just in case.)

The local paper told me what I'd hoped for. Joe Rubin's band was playing at a dance hall in a Chicago suburb that night.

It was possible that the singer with the band once had been a blonde. But the Claudia I was looking for had blue eyes. This one didn't—and she wasn't wearing contact lenses.

Of course, there was no guarantee that Claudia Blair at The Red Room was the right girl. But there was only one way to find out. I headed for the airport, a directory and a cab.

I got to the nightclub in time for the first show. The curtains on the stage were drawn and, just as my drink was delivered, they parted. Claudia Blair was seated at a piano.

I liked her right off. She had a pleasant voice and a good stage presence. The life of a nightclub entertainer hadn't hardened her yet.

She finished her songs, and the curtains closed while she sat at the piano.

I waited a minute or two and went back to her dressing room. I knocked, she told me to come in.

Claudia was sitting in a chair knitting. She didn't look up as I entered. Somehow, I sensed that a new approach was needed for this girl:

"I caught the show, Miss Blair. You do a nice job."

"Thank you."

"My name is Goldfader. I'd like to get an interview."

She looked puzzled. "But I'm just a small-time nightclub singer, Mr. Goldfader. I've never cut a record or been on radio or TV. I don't think anybody's ever heard of me."

"Maybe a story will help," I said.

"What kind of story?"

"You know. Your background, training, early struggles, first break—you know the kind."

"I'm afraid I do," she said, "but I don't want any cheap publicity. If I get anyplace in this business, I'll do it on whatever talent I might have."

"I think you have a lot of talent, Miss Blair."

She brightened up at that. "But how I overcame my handicap would make much better reading, wouldn't it?"

With that, she held up her knitting and asked me to count the number of stitches she had completed. She lifted her head toward me, and let me see that her eyes were sightless.

She was blind.

"I'm sorry, I didn't know," I stammered; "there seem to be about twenty stitches."

She thanked me. I couldn't stop explaining.

"I really didn't know, Miss Blair."

"I'm sure you didn't. Not many people do. The curtain is always drawn before someone leads me off."

"Can't anything be done?" I asked.

"No. I'll always be blind." She paused. "I'll give you my home address. Come around any afternoon between one and five. I'll tell you whatever there is to tell."

Mrs. Squires' letter to Tracers Company had made no mention of her daughter's blindness. It seemed likely that she would have known. Even if the girl had still had her eyesight when she was placed with the orphanage, the periodic reports prior to her adoption would have mentioned it later. . . .

So, either Mrs. Squires had not informed us—for reasons of her own—or Claudia Blair wasn't her daughter. If she wasn't, I was at a dead end. (And she might have gone blind after adoption—but that left me nothing at all to work with.)

At one-thirty the next afternoon, I took a cab to the address Claudia had given me.

A lady came to the door and introduced herself as Jean Blair, Claudia's mother. She invited me in, saying that Claudia was expecting me, and she showed me into a pleasant, glass-walled room looking out onto a patio.

Claudia was sitting there, dressed in casual clothes, in contrast to her evening gown of the previous night. She looked more pretty than glamorous.

Mrs. Blair excused herself, saying that she would be in the kitchen if needed.

"Isn't she wonderful!" Claudia said. "Sometimes I think it's harder on her than me. Every mother has great hopes for her children. I was an only child, you know . . . mother had given up all hope of having a family . . . she was nearly forty when I came along."

With that, I started to get the sinking feeling that I was on the wrong track with this girl, too—the last wrong track.

Claudia went on: "Oh, sure, I can sing for a living —but I'm still dependent. It's not a happy feeling to know that you're a burden."

I was still fighting that sinking feeling, and quietly managed to say: "I'm sure you're exaggerating . . . " when Claudia, seeming not to hear me, went on:

"I'm adopted, you know. Though of course, how would you know? Anyhow, my mother gave me away when she discovered that I was going blind."

Locating Claudia wasn't difficult and it had required no particularly difficult effort. But it turned out to be only half the job. Claudia's bitterness toward her mother was obvious every time she spoke of her. She knew nothing about Mrs. Squires' whereabouts or circumstances, and made it clear she didn't want to. I felt certain she would have rejected any suggestion for a meeting with her mother.

I went back to my hotel and placed a call to Mrs. Squires. I told her of her daughter's feelings . . . and apparently it was no surprise to Mrs. Squires that Claudia had lost her sight. She requested that I make an effort to persuade Claudia to meet with her at least once.

"I'll have to talk to her adoptive parents, Mrs. Squires. . . . Yes, if they agree, I'll see what I can do. But you'll have to understand one thing: if she refuses to see you, there's nothing more to be done. . . . All right, Mrs. Squires. Good-bye."

I had nothing to do that night, so I went to The Red Room to see Claudia perform, but I didn't let on that I was there. Before her first song was over, I left and headed for her home.

Mrs. Blair greeted me at the door and immediately explained that Claudia was working.

"I know. I came to talk to you."

"Oh . . . come in, please."

We entered the den, where Claudia's father was reading the newspaper. Mrs. Blair introduced me as the man who had come to interview Claudia.

Mr. Blair asked me how the story was going.

"I'm sorry, sir. I'm not a writer. I'm an investigator and I trace missing persons."

Mrs. Blair gasped. "Oh, no! After all these years—"

I told her that Claudia's mother had been looking for most of those years, though she had hired Tracers Company only a few days earlier.

Mr. Blair wanted to know whether I had traced Claudia through the orphanage. I assured him that they'd refused to give out any information.

"Claudia is our legally adopted daughter," Mrs. Blair said, "We don't have to agree to letting her see her natural mother."

"I understand that, Mrs. Blair. So does Mrs. Squires. But she would like to see Claudia. I'm sure you understand."

"I don't think Claudia wants to see her," Mrs. Blair told me.

Mr. Blair said, "We want you to know that we haven't tried to turn Claudia against her real mother. If she seems cold or bitter toward her it's because of what she remembers. Maybe it's distorted, but she was only eight years old when she was left at the orphanage. We never knew the circumstances, but we felt that there must have been a reason."

"There usually is," I said.

"There were reasons on our side, too," Mrs. Blair added. "We went to the orphanage to adopt a baby. But there was Claudia, going on nine years old . . . and no mother or father . . . and slowly losing her eyesight. We *had* to take her. And we've never regretted it."

Mr. Blair said, "We couldn't love her any more if she was our own daughter."

"Then you ought to know how her mother feels," I said.

They glanced at each other and, after a moment, Mrs. Blair, almost imperceptibly, nodded to me.

I hope my face wasn't betraying what I was feeling right at that moment.

Persuading Claudia to see her mother was a problem for a family relations counselor. I was a tracer. But, whatever Mrs. Squires' reasons were for abandoning her child, Claudia's bitterness was doing no one any good. The job was worth doing—if I could do it.

I telephoned Claudia the next afternoon and asked whether I could see her.

"Want more material for your story?"

"I'm not a writer," I admitted.

"I know," she said, "Mother told me. Why don't you just say what you have to say and get it over with?"

"All right. Will you see her?"

"No."

"I know how you feel. But maybe you're wrong."

"I was given away!" she exploded. "When I most needed a mother, she deserted me—because she didn't want the burden of a blind child. I'll never forgive that."

"You might hear her side of it."

"Do you think there's anything she can say that will change the fact that she didn't want me? I'm sorry," she added. "This is probably an important case to you."

"I've missed before," I told her. "I didn't want this case in the first place, knowing how things like this can turn out. But every now and then, I see the good that can come of a job and it makes it worth the effort."

"Do you think any good could come from my meeting *her?* Knowing the way I feel?"

"I'd drop it if I didn't."

There was a long pause. "I'm home afternoons from one to five. Call me when she arrives."

And she hung up.

I telephoned Mrs. Squires. She said she and her husband would fly to Los Angeles that night and they would call my hotel upon their arrival. I told them I'd bring Claudia to them the next afternoon. Then I called Mr. and Mrs. Blair and they agreed that it would be best for all if Claudia visited her mother at the hotel.

The next day, at one o'clock, I called for Claudia, and our cab headed for the Biltmore, where Mr. and Mrs. Squires were staying.

As we crossed the lobby toward the elevators, a man stopped us. "I'm John Squires," he said. "I decided I'd only be in the way up there. But I did want to say hello to you, my dear."

"Thank you," Claudia said.

"Room seven ninety-five." And Mr. Squires excused himself.

Claudia and I took the elevator to the seventh floor and, as we walked toward room 795, I told Claudia to phone the desk when she was ready to leave, so that I could come up to get her.

"No," she said. "I want you to come with me. I want to talk with her, and afterwards you can tell me what she looks like. Because I won't go through it again. Once will have to be enough."

I knocked on the door and we entered the room. Mrs. Squires was seated, and remained so as we approached her.

Quietly, Claudia said, "Hello."

"So many years," Mrs. Squires said. "All the things I've saved up to tell you . . . and now I can't remember any of them. You're all grown up. But the moment you spoke . . . your voice sounded almost the same as it did that night at Mrs. Payton's. You said—*Aren't you coming, Mama?*"

"Please—"

"Come here," Mrs. Squires said, extending her hand. "I want to look at you."

I led Claudia to her mother and, as we got to her, Mrs. Squires rose and placed her hands on Claudia's face, exploring it in the fashion of blind people.

"You *are* grown up . . . and so pretty," said Mrs. Squires.

"But," Claudia cried, "you can't see either."

"No," her mother said. "But I think I would have known you."

"Nobody told me," Claudia said. "If only I had known. You said you'd come back for me—and I never knew why you didn't."

By now, they were in a tearful embrace.

"I've come for you now, my darling."

"Mama, I missed you so much. . . ."

17
THE IMPOSSIBLE SITUATION

Once in a very long while, Tracers Company gets a case that really does sound like a detective story—complete with impossible situation, baffled police and the whole load of tricks.

Here's one, and the situation can be wrapped up, as it was for me when we got the case, in a single question:

How can a man wearing only green pajamas disappear from a hotel room between 2:00 A.M. and 2:15 A.M., without money, other clothing, or knowledge of the area?

It does look like one for the mystery fans, and a very strange one at that. It was also one for me, complete with a lesson tacked on to it. The lesson is a little more complicated to state, though it may be easier at the end of this story.

It goes: Don't bother with an answer until you're sure the answer isn't the question.

Right. For a while there, I didn't understand it either.

David Benson disappeared, as described, from the hotel room he and his wife were occupying in Centralia, Illinois. The year was 1959. Mr. and Mrs. Benson had gone out to Centralia to visit with their daughter, their son-in-law and the couple's two children. David Benson was fifty-seven years old. He was a bank official in a town I'll call Centreville, Vermont, and he'd been born in Centreville and lived all his life there. He had been married for thirty years, and the marriage had produced a single daughter, the same one who was now, herself, happily married in Illinois.

As material for a detective story, that set of facts seems an uninspiring collection. There is, of course, a little more.

There almost always *is* a little more.

Mr. and Mrs. Benson had driven from Centreville to Centralia, taking four days for the trip. According to Mrs. Benson, her husband had begun acting a little strangely during the drive; he seemed more nervous than usual, she said, and he also seemed to be going into a somewhat confused state, a sort of "lack of orientation," as they went on. By the time the couple reached

Centralia, Mr. Benson was almost in a state of collapse. Mrs. Benson telephoned her married daughter and got her to call a doctor, which she did.

The Bensons were registered at a hotel, and it was in their room that the doctor examined Mr. Benson. He administered some medication to the sick man, and, after a short nap, Mr. Benson awoke, feeling, he said, perfectly wonderful.

Mrs. Benson wasn't so sure; but, in spite of her worried protestations, he insisted on going right on to the planned dinner at the house of their son-in-law.

In fact, dinner seemed to go along perfectly well, and, after a few hours of conversation Mr. and Mrs. Benson returned to their hotel room. By the time they got there, Mr. Benson was beginning to look a bit confused and uncertain again, and his wife, following the instructions the doctor had given her, made her husband take two of the pills the doctor had left for him. Mr. Benson took the pills, and went to bed. Mrs. Benson, worried because he still appeared so restless, decided to stay up and keep an eye on him.

She turned on the TV and—not surprisingly—drifted very slowly off into a hazy sleep. A commercial woke her at two in the morning.

By two-fifteen she had the basic facts.

Unfortunately, they didn't make any sense.

David Benson was gone.

His eyeglasses and his watch were gone with him.

So were his green pajamas.

His robe, his slippers, his wallet, money and keys, however, remained in the room.

So did the rest of his clothing.

Mrs. Benson went downstairs in a hurry. The elevator boy told her nothing; Mr. Benson might have walked down. The Bensons' car was still where it had been left. She walked a bit, searching, and then went back to the car and started it. She did a fast but thorough canvass of an area ten blocks square, which included a couple of all-night diners.

Nothing.

Mr. Benson wasn't there.

Apparently, Mr. Benson wasn't anywhere.

Which was impossible . . . she told herself. So she went on back to the hotel and called her daughter from there. The police (called by the daughter) and the daughter arrived at the same time—3:00 A.M. They rechecked the area.

They came up with nothing whatever.

The hotel was near the edge of town. It was decided to form a search party, going out all over the area.

The next day, therefore, a contingent of police, firemen and sheriff's deputies joined with nearly two hundred fellow workers of Mr. Benson's son-in-law, and scouted the area inch by inch. Meanwhile, a helicopter did an aerial survey of a nearby creek and covered the railroad right-of-way over a ten-mile stretch.

In the middle of the afternoon, fifty high school students joined the search parties. Everything was coordinated by the chief of police, who had radio-equipped cars, walkie-talkies, a radio in the helicopter and all modern methods at his immediate disposal. As the day wore on, an old method was rung in: three bloodhounds were given a sniff of David's clothing and let loose on the hunt.

By sundown, everybody had run out of places to look.

When a baffled high schooler suggested that just maybe Mr. Benson had been spirited away by small purple Martians in invisible flying saucers—or some such notion—he sounded surprisingly plausible. After all, the word for the situation was pretty clear by then: *impossible.*

Wasn't it?

Mrs. Benson called me, and presented me with the basket of facts I've just unpacked. A lot of routine inquiries brought us equally disappointing news almost as soon as we began work on the case. For instance:

1. Mr. Benson's business affairs were perfectly in order. In fact, he was just about to earn a handsome bonus—and had known about it.

2. His personal savings and checking accounts showed no large or inexplicable withdrawals for a full year prior to the disappearance. Joint accounts were likewise in apple-pie order.

3. According to Mrs. Benson, she and her husband hadn't been fighting, or arguing, or anything of the sort. Just to clinch that one, she showed me the gold watch he had given her for her birthday—two months

before. The watch was inscribed: *"always, David."*

All right. I took a deep breath and *really* started to work.

The present—the hotel, the surrounding area, the business and bank checkups, and so on—was getting me nowhere in a hurry. If there was an answer, then somewhere a clue to that answer existed, and it could only lie in the past.

So I kept asking about David Benson's past. Had he repeatedly talked about wanting to travel to some other part of the country, some other part of the world?

Nope.

Had he ever before behaved as oddly as he had just prior to his disappearance?

Nope.

Was there anyone among his business associates he might have talked with intimately, to whom he might have confided his closest thoughts?

Nope.

Was there ever another woman in his life?

Mrs. Benson shook her head—and then stopped, and hesitated. "Another woman?" she said. I'm sure you couldn't consider her that—certainly not after thirty years. She was just a girl David was seeing when he met me. She and I were—acquaintances, I suppose you'd say. But once David and I met, he never took her out again."

Well . . . it was the only question that hadn't been answered with a flat negative. But it didn't really look wonderful. Another woman—thirty years before.

On the other hand, I told myself, it was a lead. Not only that, it was the only lead I had.

So I went to work on it.

It seemed that the Bensons had stayed friends with this "other woman" in a limited sort of way—at any rate, Mrs. Benson said she'd had a Christmas card from the woman every year. "In fact, she called us this past year," Mrs. Benson added. "From somewhere down South, I believe it was . . . sounding a bit drunk. She said she was at a party, you see, and she—mentioned something about a double celebration: Christmas and her divorce."

Well, if that was what I had, that was what I was going to work with. And it sounded, at least, promising—in a very vague sort of way. If I could only figure out, I told myself, *how* the disappearance had been managed. . . .

While I was trying to do that, I got to work tracing the "other woman." Thirty years before, unmarried, her name had been Alice Wilson. She and Mrs. Benson had gone to the same college (where David Benson had met them both), and the college Registrar's records gave me the names and the address of her parents.

They'd moved, and the girl's father had died in the intervening years. But Mrs. Wilson, I discovered after some further checking, was living with her married daughter in Asbury Park. So I called the married daughter—who was not Alice, but Alice's younger sister.

Alice, the sister told me, was living in Pensacola. She gave me the telephone number down there.

Connecting the number to an address was easy. Connecting the address—a house with private grounds, on a private street—with anything else was going to be a little harder. There are undoubtedly thousands of ways to handle the situation, but that one time I was handed a piece of luck.

You see, normally, I don't like surveillance work: if the subject of the search is alerted, the whole case is blown right there. But (on quite a different matter) I'd had to set up a contact in Pensacola the year before, a man who was qualified for surveillance. And he had a brother-in-law who drove a milk route.

Out of the possible thousands of ways, I'd been handed a simple one. The street where David Benson's one-time girlfriend lived was on that milk route.

The next day, my man took over the route, rang the doorbell of that private house, and presented his bill. At the kitchen table, sitting and drinking coffee, was a man who seemed to be between fifty-five and sixty years old. He was wearing green pajamas.

In finding the "other woman," and thus locating David Benson, I'd worked out a *how* for that impossible disappearance; I saw that much as soon as I took a look at the facts.

The answer, of course, was the question itself. Everyone concerned, including me, had been asking it—just a little bit wrong.

The proper question was just a bit longer. It went:

How can a man wearing only green pajamas disappear from a hotel room between 2:00 A.M. and 2:15 A.M., without money, other clothing, or knowledge of

the area—*without contacting someone he knows?*
 (The "other woman" had met him in Centralia.)
 Answer:
 He can't.
 And he didn't.

EPILOGUE

The stories I've told, of the cases in which I've been involved, have ranged over about twenty years, and some of them go back nearly to the beginning of that time-span. I've picked a few out of an enormous number of cases, and told them because they seem to be good stories, they seem, sometimes to have something important to say, and—just maybe—they answer that question I started with: How do you know?

But of course the stories aren't over. There is still something new waiting for me every day, when I pick up the phone, when a client opens the door of my office. . . .

The work still fascinates me, and every day I learn a little more about it. And the work still goes on. As witness, for instance, these letters. . . .

1/10/70

Dear Sir,

I am really desparate and am writing because I must have help.

My husband left home for a business trip to New York June 18, 1969 and has never returned. I have not heard from him nor has anyone else.

I would like to know if you accept this kind of case, how much you charge, and how long it would take to find him.

I am desparately worried and am quite anxious to find him. I would appreciate hearing from you as soon as possible.

Sincerely,

Cleveland 44106, Ohio
January 14th, 1970

My Dear Mr. Edward Goldfader,

I'm a great television fan and watching Art Linkletter and son one day, I happened to see you. So I wondered at my age was there any hope for me. What I mean is I'm to be 49 this year if its the Lords will and I still don't know who or whom my parents were, and I guess I never will. But its just that feeling of just not knowing. And every person has a parent some where, mine might even be dead but like I said its just not knowing.

Just let me know what you have to know about me and I'll fill you in with what little I can tell you. If not, thanks anyway.

January 3, 1970

Mr. Edward Goldfader
Tracers Company of America
New York, New York

Dear Sir:

I recently heard of your firm and am wondering if you could help me. My husband abandoned me and my children, 6 days before my baby was born. He left for work one day and never returned. I know he is alive and well, because from time to time he sends a "conscience" card, so he can live with himself a little longer.

Could you help track him down? Please let me know what your fee is, and any information needed.

Sincerely,

London, E.6
6th November, 1969

Dear Sir,

I have been in touch with the American Embassy in London and they advised me to contact you in connection with the tracing of my brother. The details of which are as follows.

He was born in 1910 or 1911 and named ▓▓▓▓. His mother's maiden name was ▓▓▓▓ who is now deceased and the Fathers' name was ▓▓▓▓ who died about 1910. I was born July 1908 and named ▓▓▓▓

The birth place of myself and my brother was Philadelphia.

Owing to the fact that my mother was widowed and desparately short of money she put my brother into an orphanage in Philadelphia about 1910 or 1911 and my mother and I travelled to London.

It was just before my mother died that she revealed to me the facts as written.

I hope this information will be sufficient for you to be able to work upon, and I look forward to hearing from you in the near future.

Yours faithfully,

Dear Mr. Goldfader,

Robert came back from Fla. on a Honda 90 miles an hour to be reunited with his family.

He had been searching too, but nothing to work on, he was very unhappy with his adoptive parents, the boy is elated.

We are flying down Friday to be with him.

Thank you from the bottom of our hearts.

Sincerely,

TRACER! The Search for Missing Persons
This book was designed by Kay McRee. The type was set by Creative Ad Typographers, Van Nuys, California in 11 point press roman with 2 point leading on the IBM Selectric Composer. The display type is 18 pt. Microgramma Light. The printing was done by offset lithography by Publishers Press, Salt Lake City, Utah. The text stock is 60 lb. Antique and the jacket paper is 80 lb. Roughback Enamel, supplied by Publishers Press. The book is bound in Permalin Products Corporation's Permacote, by Mountain States Bindery, Salt Lake City, Utah.